Day by Day: Life, Liberty, and Joy

A Daily Dose for Daily Living

90-Day Devotional Journey

Trailon D. Johnson

Day by Day: Life, Liberty, and Joy

A Daily Dose for Daily Living

90-Day Devotional Journey

Trailon D. Johnson

Scripture quotations are from The Holy Bible, English Standard Version® (ESV®), copyright © 2001 by Crossway. Used by permission. All rights reserved.

ISBN 13: 978-1533036094
ISBN 10: 1533036098

Edited by Diane Simmons Dill, *Right*Write Productions LLC, and Angela Skelton, The Polished Nib.
www.facebook.com/rightwriteproductions and *www.facebook.com/polishednib.*

Cover design, interior design, and formatting by Diane Simmons Dill.

Cover artwork: Stock ID 1031201, *www.pixabay.com.* Used by permission.
Author's photo: Leslie Henderson Photography. Used by permission.

PRINTED IN THE UNITED STATES OF AMERICA.

Table of Contents

Introduction

The heart is deceitful above all things,
and desperately sick;
who can understand it?—Jeremiah 17:9

St. Augustine of Hippo once penned, "Our hearts are restless until they find rest in thee."[1] Or as Jeremiah asserts, the heart is desperately sick because it is so deceitful. The purpose of this book is to offer God's "prescription" for healing our sick hearts—his Holy word. Only by reading and applying God's word are we able to receive healing while striving to become more like Jesus. A closer look at this amazing organ, the heart, yields deep insights when viewed through the lens of God's precious pearls of wisdom.

The heart is one of the most vital and essential organs of the human body. According to the Centers for Disease Control and Prevention, approximately 610,000 people die every year due to heart disease.[2] More specifically, one in every four deaths is attributed to heart disease. In fact, heart disease is recorded as the leading cause of death in both men and women. This is an epidemic, not only from a medical standpoint, but also from a spiritual perspective.

Our world is plagued with spiritual heart disease; people suffer, barely holding on to life. Many carry the title "Christian" but live in bondage to sin, unsure of how to obtain the authentic, life-altering freedom found only in Christ. Some people live with heart blockages, such as holding on to past hurts, pains, and regrets, neglecting purity and living in bondage to a culture steeped in moral relativism. As a result, our identities, marriages, relationships, and our churches are struggling to survive and are in critical condition. When living in this manner with sin as our master, we are prone to a spiritual heart attack, and this type of lifestyle will eventually become detrimental to our walk with the Lord.

One of the biggest challenges facing our world is narcissism. There is a constant drive and pursuit of *OUR* dreams, desires, and passions fueled by feelings that can deceive.

This daily pursuit of "happiness," can lead to the loss of life, liberty, and joy found only in Jesus Christ. When you live with this truth, the ultimate goal is not to produce an existential reality, but to put your life in the hands of the one who created you in his image and likeness (Gen. 1:26-27). Life demands so much from us, but becoming too busy "doing" leads to a failure to "be."

However, there is good news: when you turn your life over to Christ and submit to his word, he takes the scalpel and becomes your heart surgeon. He performs open heart surgery and begins to circumcise your heart and remove the blockages so that it can function the way God designed. Finding rest for our souls is essential, and that can happen only when we walk *daily* with Jesus. The prophet Jeremiah says, "Thus says the Lord: 'Stand by the roads, and look, and ask for the ancient paths, where the good way is; and walk in it, and find rest for your souls'" (Jer. 6:16). It is my prayer that this daily devotional will serve as a supplement to your daily intake of God's word; moreover, may it be the springboard that propels you to hunger for God's word and, consequently, to live a fruitful life for the glory of God.

Yet the LORD set his heart in love on your fathers and chose their offspring after them, you above all peoples, as you are this day. Circumcise therefore the foreskin of your heart, and be no longer stubborn.—Deuteronomy 10:15-16

Week 1: Days 1~7

Day 1: Sunday's Celebration:

> *Shout for joy in the LORD, O you righteous!*
> *Praise befits the upright. Give thanks to the LORD*
> *with the lyre; make melody to him with the*
> *harp of ten strings!—Psalm 33: 1-2*

Passionate Praise

We all are passionate about something. It is amazing how exuberant and vocal participation in various sporting events, social gatherings, or political debates can be. The same is true when engaging on social media and beyond. On the other hand, when this type of excitement is directed toward our faith in Christ, believers are often ridiculed or even mocked. We should not allow the critics' voices to control us. This Psalm gives us a command to shout for joy. This is proper and suitable for those who are believers. It is not only a call to praise our God but also an invitation to use instruments to express the goodness of God. Because of Christ, there is so much to be excited about. When entering the house of the Lord today, go with the purpose of glorifying our Creator, our King. Sing hymns of praise in response to the goodness and greatness of our God (Eph. 5:19). Worship the Savior today, and celebrate Christ the King! Praise Father, Son, and Holy Ghost!

A Prayer to Start Your Week:

> *Lord, as I enter your house of worship, prepare my heart and mind to hear from you. I ask that you remove every barrier that will prevent me from engaging in wholehearted worship and submission. Let me never leave your presence without experiencing you. Lord, you alone are worthy of all worship and praise. I want more of you; I want to see you lifted high and glorified today and forevermore. In Jesus' name, Amen.*

Day 2: Monday's Motivation:

*Finally, be strong in the Lord and
in the strength of his might.—Ephesians 6:10*

True Strength

The best way to train for a sport, contest, or other performance is to be consistent, both in method and in devoting time and effort. One of the biggest setbacks among people in our world is inconsistency. Many people start but fail to finish. God did not call us to only start, but also to be a finisher. People sometimes feel as if they don't have the support, encouragement, or resources they need to complete the task that is set before them. But Paul is encouraging the church on how to be spiritually prepared—he assures us of one thing: there is a constant war, but Christ offers victory (Eph. 6:12-13). Let us be fully equipped and prepared to fight against the evil one. The power of sin and darkness has been broken, but that does not mean the enemy won't attack. Our strength comes from the Lord, through his power and his word (2 Cor. 10:3-6). No matter the test or trial, the real challenge is to trust the Savior even in our weakness. He is our rock, our strength, our shield, and our example. He endured the cross so that we would have the power to carry our crosses this week. In spite of challenges, seek to trust him wholeheartedly. As noted in Dr. Lyle Dorsett's book, *Serving God and Country,* "Battles are won by military power, but wars are won by spiritual power."[3]

A Closer Look:

1. Make a list of your strengths and weaknesses: How have these things shaped your life?

2. Are there some things you have started but not finished? How can you get back on track?

3. Think and reflect on your life. Are there places where you need the strength of the Father?

Day 3: Tuesday's Treasure:

*The grass withers, the flower fades, but the
word of our God will stand forever.*—Isaiah 40:8

Changing, Yet Consistent

I have some surprising and startling news. Things never stay the same! Seasons change; we get older, taller, bigger, and sometimes smaller. Our favorite sports teams win games and lose games. We start school, graduate, begin a career, and retire. People come into our lives and people leave our lives, but the only thing that is sure is the consistency of God's word in the midst of life's inconsistencies. In this particular verse from the prophet Isaiah, God's mouthpiece, he shares that in the midst of uncertainties, God's plan is sure. Life on earth is here today and gone tomorrow; however, God's word is final even in the fickleness. His word stands true in the tragedy, and remains permanent in the pain (Matt. 5:18). Wow, is that not great news? God's word is a treasure of rich gems and the roadmap that will inevitably chart our course and renew our souls and minds (Ps. 119:105). When this treasure is embraced, our lives take on new meaning and purpose. Today, begin by standing on the truth that will never falter—God's word. Deepen your faith today by his word, and experience his unchanging and infinite promises.

A Closer Look:

1. What are some ways you can ask God to help you adapt to change?

2. Is it hard for you to trust God's word in the midst of this fast-paced society?

3. Why is it hard to remain consistent when you are bombarded with change and difficult situations?

Day 4: Wednesday's Weapon:

*"The LORD will fight for you, and
you have only to be silent."—Exodus 14:14*

Fight Right

We often tend to take things into our own hands and try to change them when a situation or obstacle lies before us. In search of validation and acceptance, our focus shifts from God to other sources of peace, or we find ourselves trying to figure out the "why." Just as the children of Israel were on the edge of crossing the Red Sea, and the army sought to destroy them, Moses reminds them not to fear, but to remain strong and have faith (Ex. 14:13). This call to boldness and authenticity in the faith stands as a constant reminder to God's people. The best way to fight is to remain obedient to the Lord, marching to his drumbeat. Society tells us to make decisions based on our feelings. However, if our emotions guide us, we end up following our feelings, causing us to vacillate in our faith. God's way is always better, so he should lead, and we should follow him. We serve the undefeated one, and victory is always within reach when we're walking with the Lord (Ps. 24:8). Begin today by listening clearly and turning from the things that become a barrier to hearing from God. Adopt this posture to engage in the battle God's way, ultimately leading to victory.

A Closer Look:

1. Have you experienced situations that placed a barrier between you and your relationship with God?

2. Are you more prone to pray or talk to others concerning the issues you may encounter?

Day 5: Thursday's Truth:

> *Trust in the LORD forever, for the LORD GOD*
> *is an everlasting rock.—Isaiah 26:4*

Trust At Its Best

There are so many things that appear to be worthy of our trust. A bank account, a favorite sports team, getting the scholarship, and for some, the perfect job or spouse, but ultimately these things are uncertain and can let us down. It can be a challenge to completely trust in Christ alone, but he will never let us down. Trust in a system or an individual can lead to disappointment. These decisions can cause us to lose all hope, but not so fast! No matter what life looks like today or what tomorrow brings, remember to hold on to the everlasting Rock—Jesus Christ. Stay focused on him for peace, and depend upon the one who shelters and guides (Ps. 32:7). Begin the day by making the decision to stand on the everlasting Rock. Make this a personal prayer today, "Lord, I trust in you. I believe your promises are true, and I dare not depend on people or this world to do what only you, Lord, can do." The old hymn, "My Hope Is Built," describes the kind of trust in God that all believers should strive for:

> My hope is built on nothing less
> than Jesus' blood and righteousness;
> I dare not trust the sweetest frame,
> but wholly lean on Jesus' name;
> On Christ the solid rock, I stand;
> all other ground is sinking sand.[4]
>
> —Edward Mote

A Closer Look:

1. What are some areas in your life that you need to submit to the Lord?

2. Do you find it difficult to trust in God? If so, why?

Day 6: Friday's Freedom:

For we are his workmanship, created in Christ Jesus
for good works, which God prepared beforehand,
that we should walk in them.—Ephesians 2:10

Created with Purpose

As Paul addresses the church at Ephesus, he reminds them that their lives are a result of what Christ has done for them since before the beginning of time, and how they are to respond as believers. In all honesty, there have been times in our lives where hard work goes unnoticed and the fruits of our labor are unappreciated. Study and preparation did not prevent failing the test, or our prayers and petitions seem to fall on deaf ears and God seems far away. Living our lives for the sakes of others and following popular culture can hijack and hinder us from being whom God created us to be. We must never forget that we are called to live for an audience of one. Because of our relationship with Christ and our love for him, we are compelled to obey him and serve others, not to earn our salvation, but as a result of our salvation (James 2:17-18). Our lives and good works are a result of God's Spirit at work within us as it produces fruit that will change the lives of others. Adversity can be disheartening, so reach out to someone who is hurting, broken, or confused, and share the love of Christ. Opportunities to bless and serve others are all around if we only look for them. Rather than looking to receive today, give because Christ surrendered all he had, even his life. As a follower of Christ, embrace the purpose for which you were created and serve others while seeking to advance God's kingdom.

A Closer Look:

1. What does it mean to be created for God's purpose?

2. What does it mean to be created for "good works," and what does that look like in your life?

3. What are the motives behind your good deeds?

Day 7: Saturday's Strength

> *"Be still and know that I am God. I will be*
> *exalted among the nations, I will be exalted*
> *in the earth!"—Psalm 46:10*

Rest

Take a deep breath. Inhale. Now, exhale. The week is over. For some, it may seem as if work never comes to an end, but in spite of where we may find ourselves, it's important to be still and reflect on the goodness of our God. It is easy to become so "busy" that we fail to simply rest. The demands at home, work, and school can inundate our lives until slowly but surely God is edged out, and our focus begins to fade and fall away. Total happiness will never be found in people, places, and popularity, because these areas of supposed wholeness are trivial. Reflect upon this Psalm and find rest in God. He is our guide, our hiding place, and our shield (Ps. 28:8). He will be exalted among the nations and exalted in the earth. Recognize how good and powerful our God is. Rather than presenting a laundry list of the things for God to fix in your life, ask him to renew your mind and heart. When your focus on him becomes a way of life, you will begin to realize how much greater God is than your problems. Today, simply ask, and God can recharge your faith, renew your spirit, and give you a fresh start as you remain focused on him.

A Closer Look:

1. What are some areas in your life that you need to surrender to the Lord?

2. Are there times when your issues seem to be so big that they drown out the voice of God?

3. What brings you the most happiness? Why?

Week 2: Days 8~14

Day 8: Sunday's Celebration:

How lovely is your dwelling place, O LORD of hosts!
My soul longs, yes, faints for the courts of the LORD;
my heart and flesh sing for joy to the living God.—Psalm 84:1-2

The Power of His Presence

"I just need to get away!" This phrase is uttered by those who are tired of their current environment and desperately desire a breath of fresh air. Work is stressful, school is taxing, the kids are demanding, and the happenings in the world are discouraging, stripping away our peace and joy. Life sometimes has negative circumstances that cause us to complain, but what would it change? The Psalmist tells us that there is something special about entering the house of worship. Joy, peace, and strength flood our souls in the presence of the Lord (Ps. 16:11). Today, desperately desire to spend time with the Lord. Pray that this time will lead to renewal, strength, and celebration. God's authentic presence flows outwardly, and we encounter him in a powerful way. Sing praises to the Lord, but do not allow this celebration to be predicated solely upon a favorite song, but rather upon the goodness of Jesus Christ, our Savior.

A Prayer to Start Your Week

Lord, I am grateful for your presence. I stand in awe of your wonder and majesty. You are the God, the Creator and sustainer of all things. You placed the stars, moon, and sun in their rightful places. You know me by name. Lord, let me experience your presence and be encouraged and transformed by your Gospel. In my weakness, you are strong; in my doubts, you are merciful. Lord, forgive me for the times I've sinned against you and your word, and against others. I want to be made new in your presence for your glory alone. In Jesus' name, Amen.

Day 9: Monday's Motivation:

> *This God—his way is perfect;*
> *the word of the LORD proves true;*
> *he is a shield for all those*
> *who take refuge in him.*—*Psalm 18:30*

The Better Way

According to *U.S. News and World Report,* "80% of New Year's resolutions fail."[5] What a tragedy. People across the globe spend hours writing down their goals and planning for the future. Whether losing weight, finding employment, becoming financially stable, building a company, or mending broken relationships, we set goals. Goals that make us better, stronger, and more equipped for what lies ahead. While that is commendable, understand that none of these things can happen effectively and consistently unless Christ is involved (Matt. 6:33). As a culture, we have lost our focus on what is really important, turning to the "self-help" industry and those in power to solve all of our problems. Instead, seek God's wisdom. He is concerned about our lives. Don't focus on the external to the point that the internal goes unchecked; in Christ there's hope for our lives! A life worth living is lived outside of ourselves, and God's plan is far better than anything man can create on his own. Jesus Christ, our Lord and Savior, submitted to the way of the Father, and we are the beneficiaries of this act of obedience. Run toward him today and discover a better way.

A Closer Look:

1. Has there been a time in your life when you believed your way was the best and only way?

2. What are some ways you can remain obedient to God?

3. Do you believe you are in God's will? If not, what steps can you take to discover his plan?

Day 10: Tuesday's Treasure

Oh, taste and see that the LORD is good!
Blessed is the man who takes refuge in him!—Psalm 34:8

Changed Appetite

After a long day at work, to come home and sit could be the most refreshing thing to do. For some of us, it's a cup of our favorite ice cream on a hot summer's day, or a tall glass of ice water after exercising or mowing the lawn. For the food connoisseurs, it's the red light that comes on at the local Krispy Kreme®, prompting a U-turn in order to consume the best intake of sugar known to mankind. For others, it's Chick-fil-A®: always consistent and appetizing no matter the time of day. Or maybe it's neither food nor dessert, but time with friends or a fun activity, such as going to the beach, hiking, or visiting family and friends. Everyone has a favorite food and dessert, and we all desire community and fun activities that can turn a sour day into a sweet day. However, these desires, although enjoyable, do not bring complete joy because the source of true satisfaction and joy is an intimate relationship with Jesus Christ. David invites us into proper focus and worship toward the only one who is deserving and worthy of our adoration. So, if it seems as though something is missing and your tank is empty, consider submitting to Christ, filtering all desires through his will. It can become so easy to live subconsciously through others, which for a moment could bring what appears to be joy, but is actually bondage. This ultimately leads to discontentment and an unfulfilled life. But Christ changes your appetite to hunger after him; therefore, in him you will experience joy, life, freedom, and complete fulfillment.

A Closer Look:

1. What in your life brings you ultimate satisfaction?

2. How can you make sure that Christ is a priority in your life?

Day 11: Wednesday's Weapon:

> *For the word of God is living and active, and sharper*
> *than any two-edged sword, piercing to the division*
> *of soul and of spirit, of joints and of marrow,*
> *and discerning the thoughts*
> *and intentions of the heart.—Hebrews 4:12*

The Right Weapon

Wow! Living. Active. Sharp. These words are piercing and powerful! They remind me of battle scenes in movies where swords clash as armies fight for victory. Military leaders employ strategies of evasion or confrontation to bring about the best result. Some soldiers are victorious, and some are broken and defeated. God's word breaks us, but rather than leaving us broken, it builds us up. While some people in our culture perceive God's word to be antiquated and irrelevant, it comforts as it confronts, and it's our standard for doctrine and practice. Be careful; the world can be convincing that people's approval and opinions can satisfy our desires. Scripture does not suggest divorcing ourselves from people, but simply indicates that our ultimate source of peace and authority should be God's word. His truths are not only comforting to those who believe, but the word of God also cuts and pierces. There's a lot we can do without, but the one thing we cannot live without is God's word. It challenges our thoughts and intentions. God honors hearts and souls that are committed to him, and his word reveals character and challenges faith. Allow the word of God to search and penetrate to renew a hardened heart and confused mind, and receive the greatest possible weapon to fight the enemy.

A Closer Look:

1. What is your first response when faced with personal obstacles and challenges?

2. How is the Gospel living and active in your life?

Day 12: Thursday's Truth:

> *"And there is salvation in no one else, for there is*
> *no other name under heaven given among men*
> *by which we must be saved."—Acts 4:12*

One Way

We live in a culture where churches are filled every week, but the idea or will to submit to God's word seems foreign. Church attendance becomes just another ritual or a check mark on a list of things to do. The desire to please the popular culture rather than pleasing God has become the more attractive and socially acceptable way. In the early church, countless men and women were persecuted for their profession of faith in Jesus Christ as Lord and Savior. It was during those times of persecution that the church grew. Peter and John were questioned and challenged by religious leaders for their unyielding and unwavering faith (Acts 4:1-11). Modern Christians can relate—for example, working for an organization whose focus is not on glorifying God, or being a student or young adult who is harassed or mocked because of their faith. Maybe a married couple is being challenged by others for promoting the biblical definition of marriage. Submitting to God's will and emulating the example of Christ supersede any social ideology. Be bold and passionate in faith, and stand for Christ. Recommit your life to the Lord every day, and allow him to direct you and show you his powerful truth. This truth, though powerful, is also simple—Jesus is the ONLY way to God the Father, salvation, and eternal life (John 14:6).

A Closer Look:

1. What are you most passionate about? Why?

2. How do you stand firm in the faith when faced with hostility and persecution?

3. Do you find it difficult to remain strong spiritually in a world that is embedded with compromise?

Day 13: Friday's Freedom:

*"Therefore do not be anxious about tomorrow,
for tomorrow will be anxious for itself. Sufficient for the
day is its own trouble."—Matthew 6:34*

What's the Point?

Is there any point to worrying, or will stressing miraculously change the situation? Worry comes in endless forms: will the dream job work out, is your dream home within reach? Will money or grades gain entrance into your desired school? After a long period of working, is retirement within your grasp? Is marriage on God's radar for you? Will your children honor God with their lives and be successful in their work? Although these are healthy concerns, remember that the Lord orders our steps and teaches us how we are called to live as his people (Ps. 37:23). Worry eats away at our faith and drags us into a pit of despair, restlessness, and uncertainty, but seeking God's kingdom and resting in his ultimate rule and reign are where hope and liberty reside. A life that is submitted to the will and purpose of God is an expression of our trust in the sovereignty of God. So, when worry creeps in, remember the powerful and reassuring words of Jesus. His promises are true and his faithfulness is everlasting. Devote time today to drawing closer to the Savior and seeking him. No matter what life presents, God graciously gives the peace that surpasses all understanding (Phil. 4:7). Embrace this peace, and avoid worrying about tomorrow by looking to Jesus, the Prince of Peace—that's the whole point.

A Closer Look:

1. What is your greatest source of worry, and how do you handle it?

2. Worry is misplaced energy and focus. Do you find yourself placing your energy and focus on Christ or on things that worry you?

3. Do you find it hard to let go and trust God?

Day 14: Saturday's Strength:

> *I will lift up my eyes to the hills.*
> *From where does my help come?*
> *My help comes from the LORD,*
> *who made heaven and earth.*—*Psalm 121:1-2*

The Ultimate Source

At some point in time, everyone will want and need help. Whether we admit it or not, no one has accomplished anything or achieved any milestone or exploit without help. No student, leader, athlete, or performer achieved success on their own. Someone walked alongside, supported, and guided them. Perhaps a parent, teacher, coach, pastor, or friend has been there to encourage us and give wisdom at the right time. Certainly, these individuals are to be commended and appreciated. However, there's a huge blind spot in our culture. There's a false hope that has been created. We have become outwardly dependent on politicians, people, and the "powerful," resulting in failure to recognize and revere the ultimate source of our help. It can become easy to trust in those who seem to have all the answers. This dependence upon others can make us forget the source of all things, Jesus Christ. The Psalmist is not confused as to where his help comes from. Instead of looking outwardly, he's focused on the Creator; recognize that we are nothing apart from God (John 15:5). Today, look to him, the all-powerful one. Your very existence is a gift of his grace and lovingkindness. Choose to recognize the reality of who he is; rest in him and find strength in the ultimate source: Jesus Christ, to whom all glory and honor belong.

A Closer Look:

1. What are some attributes of God?

2. Do you remember the last time you completely trusted in Jesus?

3. How can you demonstrate being intentional about living a life that is totally dependent upon Christ?

Week 3: Days 15~21

Day 15: Sunday's Celebration:

I was glad when they said to me,
"Let us go to the house of the LORD!"—Psalm 122:1

Somewhere Special

Some places are special. While in divinity school, I always enjoyed going into Hodges Chapel. In my years there, this sacred space became a place of prayer, worship, and renewal—it was a place where I sensed and felt the presence of God in a special way. We all have places that bring us utmost joy, where we go to retreat and get away from the noise. For some, it is summer excursions to the beach or lake, while others enjoy visiting a theme park or a museum on a hot summer's day. On the other hand, places can be reminders of a horrid past that keeps one arrested by fear and torment. Throughout my ministry, I have spoken with several people who feel that certain places were an incubator of steady pain and rejection. However, the place that David speaks of is one of joy, peace, and expectation. David finds joy in going into the house of the Lord. There's something special about gathering to worship Jesus. Corporate worship is important because it creates a unified community that is equipped to do the work God has called us to do (Eph. 4:11-13). Today, go with joy, expecting not only to receive from God, but to give and worship the only one worthy of honor and glory, Jesus Christ, our God. A place of worship can be the most special place of all.

A Prayer to Start Your Week

Lord, allow my eyes to remain fixed on you and your promises in spite of my present pains, and let me worship you with an eternal perspective as I gather with the body of Christ. Help me remember to keep you high and lifted up so that every day is special. Above all, help me to maintain a heart of worship and praise. In Jesus' name, Amen.

Day 16: Monday's Motivation:

"Have I not commanded you? Be strong and courageous.
Do not be frightened, and do not be dismayed, for the LORD
your God is with you wherever you go."—Joshua 1:9

Assurance

What an awesome promise and assurance concerning the faithfulness of our God. Throughout Scripture prior to Joshua, God showed his covenantal love and faithfulness to Noah, Abraham, Isaac, Jacob, and Moses, and this promise was extended to Joshua (Ex. 3:6, Josh. 1:5). God promised to never leave him, and his word still stands true. However, life can throw curve balls, push us off course, and make us doubt God's word. As Joshua began his mission, God gave specific instructions on how to be successful. God warned against being fearful or discouraged. Being fearful can demonstrate itself in taking the easy, less strenuous path, but sometimes it's traveling the difficult and treacherous roads that strengthens and matures us. But the great thing about our God is that he goes before us, aware and concerned when we become discouraged and fearful. God did not want Joshua to become embedded with doubt, but to be empowered with truth. As God was with Joshua, God promises to be with you. Do not be fearful of encountering discouraging moments. Instead, be encouraged and see it as an opportunity to flex your faith "muscles." Strengthening your faith provides the courage to rest in the truth that you are not alone; our covenant God is faithful, and he is with you. Draw close to him today, confident of his promise of assurance.

A Closer Look:

1. Do you experience difficulty in realizing that you can find rest in Christ in the midst of the unexpected?

2. Can you think of ways to honor God's commandment to be strong and fearless in spite of the circumstances?

Day17: Tuesday's Treasure

So God created man in his own image,
in the image of God he created him;
male and female he created them.—Genesis 1:27

God's Blueprint

God is the Creator and sustainer of the entire Universe and everything in it (Ps. 24:1-2). In the book of Genesis we learn that he created both male and female and gave them dominion to rule and reign as his representatives. Male and female have equal value and significance while remaining unique and distinct so that they might fulfill God's divine purpose on earth. Adam and Eve had perfect intimacy with the Father, and God's divine order is for one male and one female to unite together and to multiply. Our calling is to bring glory to God with our lives. In a world that seeks to redefine marriage and taint God's original design, one thing is certain—God's word is final, and it will never change (Matt. 24:35). As God's representatives, we are called to show what honoring marriage and unity are all about (Gen. 2:18, Eph. 5:22-33). God's plan and design for marriage is far more fulfilling and rewarding than anything we could create or develop on our own. As God's representative, commit to submitting to his blueprint, and lead others to do the same.

A Closer Look:

1. Do you recognize your value and worth as an image bearer of God?

2. What do you believe is important to consider as you prepare yourself for marriage God's way?

3. According to God's blueprint, what are some ways you can love and encourage others into embracing healthy relationships?

Day 18: Wednesday's Weapon:

"Everyone then who hears these words of mine and does them will
be like a wise man who built his house on the rock.
And the rain fell, and the floods came, and the winds blew and beat
on that house, but it did not fall, because it had been founded on
the rock. And everyone who hears these
words of mine and does not do them will be
like a foolish man who built his house on the sand.
And the rain fell, and the floods came, and the
winds blew and beat against that house,
and it fell, and great was the fall of it."—Matthew 7:24-27

Built to Last

For anyone who has ever lived in Louisiana, hurricanes are a part of life. Between engulfing waters and boisterous winds, the damage to homes and lives can be massive. Not everyone has experienced a hurricane, but we have all experienced storms in our lives that were not predicted, expected, or invited. Jesus gives us a panoramic picture and understanding of the difference between the wise and foolish builder. One who hears the word yet doesn't heed it invites a life with a faulty foundation that becomes wrapped in deception. Perhaps they simply do not realize the value of living out God's word. Sadly, this seems to be the rhythm of many lives. As believers, we are called to be wise builders and live out the truths of Scripture (James 1:22-25). Seek to have open ears and an open heart to the Living God's wisdom and the desire to know him more. When this is your desire, God's word will provide a strong foundation that can stand against the waves and winds of life.

A Closer Look:

1. Do you believe following instructions is easy or difficult?

2. Have you ever found yourself in a predicament where you knew doing the right thing was the best decision but found it hard to follow through?

3. What can you do to make sure your life is built on Christ and not on the culture around you?

Day 19: Thursday's Truth

*In this you rejoice, though now for a little while, if necessary,
you have been grieved by various trials so that the tested
genuineness of your faith—more precious than gold that
perishes though it is tested by fire—may be found to result in
praise and glory at the revelation of Jesus Christ.—1 Peter 1:6-7*

Fireproof

Experiencing pain is inevitable. Christ never told us that we would live a pain-free life, but he promised that resting in him would give us peace (John 16:33). One of life's biggest challenges is internal peace, primarily because we tend to focus on external conditions and momentary experiences. When our focus is on self-gratification outside the presence of God, we eventually waste away internally. Becoming a follower of Christ does not make life easier; in some ways, it becomes more challenging, but the blessing is that Christ walks with us (Deut. 31:6). Trials strengthen us, and we are called to praise God in life's valleys! When faced with life-altering circumstances, lean into the Savior and experience healing, hope, and joy. Today, live with eternity in view, knowing that the present reality is nothing compared to what is to come (Rom. 8:18-25). As C.S. Lewis states in his book, *Mere Christianity,* "If I find in myself a desire which no experience in this world can satisfy, the most probable explanation is that I was made for another world."[6] With this promise, you can stay strong, even when walking through the fire.

A Closer Look:

1. Can you think of anything that has robbed you of your peace?

2. How can you be intentional in making Christ the center of your peace?

3. Read Romans chapter 8. What do you learn about Paul concerning walking according to the Spirit and his perspective on suffering?

Day 20: Friday's Freedom:

> *If then you have been raised with Christ,*
> *seek the things that are above, where Christ is,*
> *seated at the right hand of God.*
> *Set your minds on things that are above,*
> *not on things that are on earth.—Colossians 3:1-2*

Reality Check

Tired? Confused about life? The light at the end of the tunnel is nowhere to be found? Know that there's hope in Jesus Christ. Paul shares with the church the unique union between them and Christ, a union that still exists today. Singular focus on what is around us can lead to discouragement and defeat; but the faithfulness and power of Christ offers rest through the Holy Spirit. This enables us to stand firm despite our current reality. What we view as reality on earth is far from the reality of eternity. Remaining cognizant of the fact that reality is awaiting us in heaven can lessen any upsetting "realities" in our earthly lives. Trust in the finished work of Christ, the exalted one who holds the primary position of honor, power, and majesty (Heb. 1:3-9). Any darkness in our lives becomes bright when the light of Christ enters, opening our eyes to his reality, the reality of freedom and victory through him. The well-known hymn, "O, For a Thousand Tongues to Sing," sums up this reality:

> He breaks the power of canceled sin,
> he sets the prisoner free;
> his blood can make the foulest clean,
> his blood availed for you and for me.[7]
> —Charles Wesley

A Closer Look:

1. Do you find it difficult to focus on God's word? What steps are you taking to refocus?

2. Can you think of ways to help you realign your thoughts?

Day 21: Saturday's Strength:

*A wise man is full of strength, and a man
of knowledge enhances his might.—Proverbs 24:5*

Lasting Legacy

One of the highlights of my life was traveling to Alsen, Louisiana to visit my great-grandfather. This was such a life-giving atmosphere; at the age of 104, he embodied decades of Godly wisdom and character. This was not only spoken, but also demonstrated through his life. His endurance and tenacity to withstand the racial injustices and hardships of life, yet remaining steadfast, was remarkable. As a result, my life was encouraged and empowered because of his strength and wise counsel. Knowledge and experience were certainly important and valuable, but the heart of his wisdom was founded on a genuine relationship with Jesus Christ. As I read these words penned by Solomon, I can't help but think about the Godly legacy we are called to live and pass on. This way of life enables us to be effective in witnessing for his kingdom because it imparts the ability to make Christ-honoring decisions. True wisdom is filtered through abiding in God's word and a growing relationship with the Lord (John 15:7). Ask God for guidance in choosing Godly women or men who can impart spiritual truths. Modern society depends upon computers, the internet, and social media to communicate. But early Christians primarily had only word of mouth and the elders' teachings; it worked beautifully to spread the Gospel. In the same way, you are called to reach out, person-to-person, in order to further the cause of Christ and leave a legacy that will last, not only for the present, but also throughout eternity.

A Closer Look:

1. What do you think it means to leave a spiritual legacy?

2. What type of legacy do you want to pass on to your children and/or to those in your sphere of influence?

Week 4: Days 22~28

Day 22: Sunday's Celebration:

I will give thanks to the LORD with my whole heart;
I will recount all of your wonderful deeds.—Psalm 9:1

Attitude of Gratitude

Growing up, I was taught to say "thank you" when someone did something for me. Those words have forever been written on the tablets of my heart and etched in my mind as I reflect upon what it means to be thankful. Sadly, this is becoming a lost virtue in our society. Satisfaction can be elusive, and we often desire more. The basis for thanks and appreciation must start with our relationship with the Lord, and David embodied such a relationship. Think about all the Lord has done for you—not only the grand exploits, but also the smaller victories that seem insignificant. The ability to see, feel, and hear are blessings we often take for granted. Our hearts should be overwhelmed with gratitude for all God has done. A heart that ceases to give thanks is one that can be blinded from an understanding of what and whom life is all about. Walk in humility and thanksgiving for the faithfulness of God (Ps. 138). God's faithfulness is sufficient to give you a heart's desire for gratitude toward him.

A Prayer to Start Your Week

Lord, what an awesome God you are. Your majesty and might are far beyond what I can think or imagine. As I reflect upon your wonderful deeds, how you created the sun, moon, and stars, and how you, by the power of the Holy Spirit, live within me, I am drawn to surrender and submit all that I am for your glory alone. Let me not become so self-centered that my heart becomes hardened, lest I forget all that you are. I need you, Lord. I can't live without your presence at work in my life. Help me to never lose the wonder and the joy that existed when I first believed. May I daily remember to keep gratitude as my attitude. In Jesus' name, Amen.

Day 23: Monday's Motivation:

Your word is a lamp to my feet
and a light to my path.—Psalm 119:105

Light for the Journey

There's nothing worse than trying to find the way through a dark room. Walking in darkness causes us to run into something, break something, or hurt ourselves or others. Not only is natural darkness dangerous and fearful, but spiritual darkness can destroy someone's life. Our country is facing spiritual darkness, infiltrating many homes, schools, and individuals' lives. When we ignore the words of Scripture, the light of Christ is hidden. Not all of us are aware when we begin walking in darkness because it has become a new normal. Our eyes have adjusted to the surroundings, making us numb and immune to the dark. There is still hope for us in the darkness, a Light shining brightly and showing us the way. Direction is found in God's word, as expressed in Psalm 25:4: "Make me to know your ways, O Lord; teach me your paths." When confused, frustrated, and unaware of what to do or where to go—dive into the Scriptures. There will be times of uncertainty, but don't lose hope in the Savior. Allow his word to be the shining light that illuminates the direction in which you keep walking.

A Closer Look:

1. Do you consider it easy or difficult to walk in the light of truth?

2. Think about a time you've been lost. How did it feel?

3. How can you be sure that Christ is leading your life?

Day 24: Tuesday's Treasure:

Let all bitterness and wrath and anger and clamor and slander be put away from you, along with malice. Be kind to one another, tender-hearted, forgiving one another, as God in Christ forgave you.—Ephesians 4:31-32

Let it Go

I believe two of the biggest silent killers, both physically and spiritually, are not forgiving transgressions and living a life with unconfessed sin. Paul informs the church of their calling and new way of life as believers. Resentment, rage, hostility, lack of self-control, or deadly words and behavior will harm our neighbors and infect our souls. Paul is calling for unity for a people as they walk in new life as followers of Christ. These traits of kindness and forgiveness should be a part of the DNA of a Christ follower. All of us have been hurt, but this does not have to be the story you subscribe to. Remember that Christ forgave all of us, so follow his example and forgive those who offend us (Matt. 6:14). Refusing to let go of what happens to you prevents the experience of freedom. You will remain locked in a prison of past pains and failures. Today, let it go. The enemy wants to rob you of your destiny, causing you to wander in the wilderness. But Christ has come to set the captives free and to give new life in him to all who call upon his name.

A Closer Look:

1. Do you find it hard to let go of past hurts and decisions?

2. Are there any past emotional wounds that are driving and controlling your life?

3. Make a list of the past or current pains, wounds, and places of unforgiveness in your life that are holding you in bondage. What steps are you taking to find freedom, and are you allowing the Lord to heal your heart and mind?

Day 25: Wednesday's Weapon:

But he would withdraw to desolate places and pray.—Luke 5:16

Secret Place

There's no better person to learn from than our Lord and Savior, Jesus Christ. After teaching and healing many diseases and afflictions, Jesus retreated for prayer to seek the Father. Prayer is one of our most important weapons and tools as believers. Without intentionality in our prayer lives, we are crippled, nearly paralyzed, and will burn out. Jesus went to the secret place to pray and seek the Father. Some people enjoy being alone, but for others, it can be one of the scariest and most intimidating things to do. Can I suggest that there is a blessing in being alone? In our modern world, separation equates to one being anti-social, unfriendly, or boring, but it's just the opposite. The need to retreat affects everyone at some point. Withdrawal from the busyness of our culture to seek the Father is important for every Christ follower. Something incredible happens when we enter the secret place and seek the Lord. Seeking others for counsel and guidance is affirmed in Scripture, but it should not serve as a substitute for quiet time with the Lord. Through prayer, we communicate with our heavenly Father, our Lord and Savior. Prayer is more than sharing our needs with God; it's praise and thanksgiving, it's reverence to our Almighty God, and it's listening to him. No formal words are needed. Just talk to the Father. He is listening. Stay in a posture of prayer; it will encourage and empower you to draw closer to the Savior because of the intimacy that prayer provides (Phil. 4:6-7). Your prayer closet is one of the best secret places to hear from the Father and grow closer to him.

A Closer Look:

1. Is prayer a priority or a second thought in your life?
2. How can you develop and foster an effective prayer life?

Day 26: Thursday's Truth:

They are to do good, to be rich in good works,
to be generous and ready to share.—*1 Timothy 6:18*

Making a Difference

Where we spend our time and money reveals what we value. The question is, are we good stewards of the resources God has blessed us with? Most Americans are not concerned about where their next meal will come from or whether they will have somewhere to sleep. According to a 2014 *USA Today* report, Americans waste $165 billion annually by throwing away unwanted food and snacks.[8] In this consumer driven society, let us not forget that our purpose is not to build bigger barns for ourselves while forgetting and neglecting the needs and concerns of those around us. We are called to help those who are in desperate need of both physical and spiritual nourishment. Across the globe, there are people who are not sure what they will eat or if they will even survive. For the comfortable, the question is not **what** we will eat, but **WHERE.** It is easy to focus on our own well-being and forsake those around us who are less fortunate. Paul instructs Timothy to inform those who are wealthy in the Ephesian church to have a spirit of generosity. America is blessed to be one of the world's most prosperous nations. The vast majority of Americans have something they can share with someone in need. Let us be good stewards of our God-given resources. Having a multitude of blessings provides an open door to go out of our way to be a blessing to our neighbors. Seek to not be consumers, but givers (Acts 20:35). It is when you give for the cause of Christ that you are satisfied and will make a difference for generations to come.

A Closer Look:

1. Can you identify essential needs in your community?

2. What are some ways you can make an impact in the lives of those around you?

Day 27: Friday's Freedom:

Whoever walks with the wise becomes wise,
but the companion of fools will suffer harm.—Proverbs 13:20

Who Are We Walking With?

The people with whom we choose to associate can, and will, shape our character in one way or another. It's good to have friends, but our desire to want should not cause us to desperately settle and compromise our values for the sake of another. King Solomon reminds us that wisdom begins by first having a reverential fear for the Lord (Prov.1:7). Fearing the Lord means to revere and honor him, which allows us to walk in loving obedience and make God-honoring decisions. We are not of this world, but we must live in the world among all kinds of people. While wisdom should be the guide in selecting close friendships, we are commanded to reach out to others, including those who do not share our faith or values. However, it's wise to evaluate the people in our lives. Do they bring us closer or farther away from the Lord? Do our relationships hold us accountable? If answering these questions is a struggle, an inventory of the weights holding us down can assist in their removal. Complete transparency with God and yourself is necessary. Then Christ can provide the freedom that comes only from him. Walk in wisdom in order to have healthy, Christ-honoring relationships.

A Closer Look:

1. What characteristics would you use to describe the "ideal" friend?

2. Are there any people in your life who hold you accountable? Do you believe Godly relationships are important?

3. What are some ways you can foster healthy and Godly relationships?

Day 28: Saturday's Strength:

The name of the LORD is a strong tower;
the righteous man runs into it and is safe.—Proverbs 18:10

I.D.

There's power in a name; it brings identity, purpose and security. The first thing we want to know when meeting someone is their name as a point of reference. People want to know about our families in general and our surnames in particular. They probe regarding whom we know because they want the familiarity and assurance of knowing what we are about and whether we have mutual acquaintances. Shared commonalities are reassuring to others that we are "ok," someone it is safe to know and associate with. Solomon tells us that the name of the Lord is a strong tower. There's purpose behind this name—the name of the Lord gives strength and protection to those who know God. We serve a faithful God, full of power, mercy, and wisdom, whose arms are open to his children, where they find safety (Ps. 46:1). Strength and security apart from Jesus Christ do not exist. Embrace the new identity you have in him as a Christ follower, and run to the safety of his arms.

A Closer Look:

1. How do you deal with your feelings when it seems as if you have no hope or security?

2. In your life, how does Christ function as your peace and comforter?

3. What are some ways you can depend upon the Holy Spirit to guide you and walk alongside you? Is this challenging for you?

Week 5: Days 29~35

Day 29: Sunday's Celebration:

> *Oh sing to the LORD a new song,*
> *for he has done marvelous things!*
> *His right hand and his holy arm have*
> *worked salvation for him.*—*Psalm 98:1*

Powerful Praise

Everyone has something to be grateful for. Life, health, the ability to see, hear, digest, just to name a few. Likewise, there can be many reasons to complain. The old saying is right, "There's always someone worse off than we are." But God has been faithful to us and has given us another opportunity to worship him today. Enter the house of the Lord and sing a new song to the God of our salvation. Let this be the jumpstart of the week. There will be those who choose to complain about how bad life is, but choose to focus on the marvelous deeds of our God. He has given us the gift of salvation through his blood that was shed on the cross. When we focus on him and the wonderful, miraculous things he has done, the experience will revolutionize our lives. His blood set us free, and it cancelled our debt. All glory, honor, and praise belong to our holy and righteous God.

A Prayer to Start Your Week

> *Lord, let me remain focused on worshipping you,*
> *my Lord and King. Let me never become so inwardly*
> *focused that I miss the wonder of your majesty. Thank*
> *you for delivering me from the bondage of sin, shame,*
> *and guilt. Today, I come before you to worship you. Let*
> *my prayer today be the impetus to a week of praise,*
> *honor, and glory to you, my Rock and Redeemer. In*
> *Jesus' name, Amen.*

Day 30: Monday's Motivation:

And let us not grow weary of doing good,
for in due season we will reap,
if we do not give up.—Galatians 6:9.

Stay the Course

Have you ever felt like giving up? Paul endured overwhelming circumstances, but he remained steadfast in the faith. In Galatians 6:8, he reminded this body of believers of the benefit of sowing into the Spirit rather than the flesh. When the purpose of our doing is centered on pleasing Jesus, then it will be worth any temporary pain we experience. God is aware, and he sees the intentions of our hearts (Prov. 17:3). Always remain faithful, and at the proper time, fruit will come forth. A tree never bears fruit immediately, but must be properly watered and nurtured. Remember, we're making an eternal difference. So, when doing good for others brings no visible results, trust God. When all resources are exhausted and no one responds, trust God. When the timing seems inconvenient and inconsistent, trust God. Stay focused on God's word and his plans. God will not show you the entire script; he just calls you to trust him and to remember that he is at work. God always does his part; your responsibility is to stay the course, grounded in faith, as you wait upon his perfect will and timing.

A Closer Look:

1. Have you ever felt like giving up? If so, is it easy for you to give up? Why?

2. Do you get discouraged when things don't happen in your ideal timing?

3. Can you think of some ways you can be more dependent upon your heavenly Father?

4. What steps can you take to persevere and not give up too quickly?

Day 31: Tuesday's Treasure:

Jesus said to them, "I am the bread of life;
whoever comes to me shall not hunger,
and whoever believes in me shall never thirst."—John 6:35

True Fulfillment

A tragedy occurs globally every night—one in every nine people goes to bed hungry, according to *The State of Food Insecurity.*[9] People have numerous needs, including physical, emotional, financial, and spiritual. As followers of Jesus Christ, we have a biblical responsibility to be intentional in caring for the least of these in our communities as well as those who are spiritually destitute (Matt. 25:35-40, James 1:27). Not only is there an epidemic from a social standpoint for the millions who lack food, but there are also individuals who are starving and malnourished spiritually. The demands of life can upset our balance and drain us of energy. Jesus proclaims that he is the bread of life. He is the one who recharges us, and he is the one who brings satisfaction and completion to our lives. Today, look to the Savior for fulfillment. He has promised to supply all of our needs (Phil. 4:19). It will not be found in drugs, alcohol, a relationship, or sex; it is found only in Jesus Christ, our King. Today, ask the Holy Spirit to fill you completely. When Jesus is all you have, he's all you need and more. Stand with arms open wide to receive all God has to offer: love, joy, peace, and his ultimate purpose. Seek the Lord with fervor because true fulfillment for every area of life is found only in Christ.

A Closer Look:

1. Have you ever been hungry? How does this make you feel emotionally, physically, and mentally?

2. Do you believe your life will be different if you live to please the Savior rather than people?

Day 32: Wednesday's Weapon:

So shall my word be that goes out from my mouth;
it shall not return to me empty, but it shall
accomplish that which I purpose, and shall succeed
in the thing for which I sent it.—*Isaiah 55:11*

Trustworthy

There was a time in history where contracts were made verbally and some by only a handshake. What people promised is what they produced. However, as years passed, honesty became something that was not commended or expected, and as we look at our modern world, this remains an unfortunate reality. The ongoing 2016 Presidential race is a perfect example as lies and underhanded tactics are reflected in the behavior of many candidates, even among those who profess to be Christians. Today, before the ink dries, contracts are broken and misused. However, be careful not to allow your view of people to become your view and perspective of God. In verse 10 the prophet Isaiah uses the consistency of rain and snow to show its ability to serve its purpose on the earth. It speaks about God's trustworthiness. What God speaks, he produces (Gen. 1). Rest in knowing that his promises will come to pass in his perfect timing; hold on dearly to the fact that God is faithful. His word functions as your greatest weapon of defense against the enemy. Use this weapon to know how to fight against the lies of Satan. God has made a promise, and it will fulfill its purpose for your good and his glory.

A Closer Look:

1. If you have ever been deceived, think back to how the deception made you feel. Have you ever been the deceiver? How do you believe it made the other person feel?

2. How would you define trust?

Day 33: Thursday's Truth:

> *"You are the light of the world. A city set
> on a hill cannot be hidden. Nor do people light a lamp
> and put it under a basket, but on a stand, and it
> gives light to all in the house. In the same way,
> let your light shine before others, so that they may
> see your good works and give glory to your
> Father who is in heaven."—Matthew 5:14-16*

Turn the Light On

Most people have a flashlight in their homes, perhaps to light the way during a power outage. Without light, we would hurt ourselves, others, and lose our way. When Jesus is the center of our lives, the Light of all lights lives on the inside of us (John 8:12). Our calling is to reflect Jesus' light in this dark and dismal world. When light shows up, darkness has to leave. As Christ delivers one of his famous sermons, the Sermon on the Mount, he continues by telling his followers they must know how they are called to function. There is hope for us and this world, and it is found in Christ. With this assurance, we are compelled to live and love as Christ has modeled for every believer. As the sun raises its brow on the break of every new day, with all its radiance and beauty, it is a reminder of the assurance of a fresh start. Christ alone is a shining Light who gives all peace, hope, and direction.

A Closer Look:

1. Have you ever had to walk in a dark room without any light? Describe this experience.

2. What does it mean for Christ to call us, his children, to be the light of the world? City on a hill?

3. What are some ways that you can be the light in this dark and dismal society and culture?

Day 34: Friday's Freedom:

And he said to him, "If your presence will not go with me,
do not bring us up from here."—Exodus 33:15

Purposeful Presence

Travel and adventures are always enjoyable, but what makes the journey exciting is not the trip itself but the people who travel with us. Family vacations have always been an essential element to my family, and we have shared several interesting and entertaining adventures. Undoubtedly, everyone will get lost at least once or twice when traveling to an unfamiliar territory. The voices of the innocent who desire to help by giving instruction and direction in a place that's unfamiliar are not always helpful. I vividly remember my mother asking before our departures, "Do you have the GPS?" The GPS was our direction and security for the journey. As I reflect on my mother's words, I can't help but think about Moses' need for guidance and protection as he and the Israelites were leaving Sinai. Moses believed that if they were to be the nation that God had destined them to be, then God's presence was vital (Ex. 33:12-14). Without God's presence, we would be unable to walk in freedom and live a life that brings glory to the Father. With God as your Guide, and his word as your roadmap, there is assurance of his peace and protection; this, my friend, can be the difference maker in all our lives (Ps. 16:11). Allow God's presence to be the ultimate GPS—God's Peace and Safety—for every aspect of life.

A Closer Look:

1. Think about the person in your life who serves as your confidant or best friend. Why is it easy to confide in them?

2. Why are instructions and guidance important?

3. In what ways have you become more dependent upon the presence of God leading you?

Day 35: Saturday's Strength:

So that Christ may dwell in your hearts through faith—that you, being rooted and grounded in love, may have the strength to comprehend with all the saints what is the breadth and length and height and depth, and to know the love of Christ that surpasses knowledge, that you may be filled with all the fullness of God.—Ephesians 3:18-19

Grounded in Love

"Love" is a word that is loosely used in our culture today, and Paul sought to express God's divine love to the church. Humans tend to prescribe love to things that cannot comprehend it and to people who may abuse it. When this occurs, it can generate confusion and leave lives and relationships broken. Love can be difficult, and our finite minds will never fully comprehend it. Love is expressed and emulated by walking with God daily. Totally experiencing and embracing the love of Christ allows us to follow him with all of our hearts, minds, and strength (Deut. 6:5). Moreover, we can love people of all ethnicities, male and female, without unhealthy motives. Love is not a thing. It is a person, a foundation that rests on the cross and resurrection of Christ. Love was broken to make you whole and resurrected to provide a destiny. In Christ, you experience the immensity and completeness of love. Today, find comfort and rest in the truth of his love. It cannot be solely explained; it must also be experienced and embraced. True love is grounded in a relationship with the epitome of love and truth, Jesus Christ.

A Closer Look:

1. How would you define love?

2. Do you believe the word "love" is loosely used in our current culture?

3. When you think about the love of Christ, does it challenge you to make changes in your life?

Week 6: Days 36~42

Day 36: Sunday's Celebration:

Oh come, let us sing to the LORD;
let us make a joyful noise to the rock
of our salvation! Let us come into his presence
with thanksgiving; let us make a joyful noise to him
with songs of praise!—Psalm 95:1-2

An Open Invitation

Invitations, expected or not, no matter the occasion, can make us feel appreciated and accepted, bringing us excitement and joy. This Psalm invites us to sing to the Lord and praise the one who is the foundation of our faith, Jesus Christ. There can be numerous reasons to be bitter and upset about life. However, don't allow broken relationships, unemployment, troubled children, or any other circumstance to cause you to lose hope. Instead, embrace the goodness of God and have a heart of gratitude. We all have countless reasons to be thankful today. He loves us, he saves us, he delivers us, and he rescues us from the depths of despair (Col. 1:13-14). Now those are great reasons to rejoice! For all that he is and all that he has done, let praise be your weapon today to fight against any depression, doubts, or frustrations. It can, and will, lift your spirit. Instead of allowing the noise of pain to discourage you, allow the joy of the Lord to be your strength (Neh. 8:10). The Lord's day offers an open invitation to praise him, an invitation that can be extended to every day.

A Prayer to Start Your Week

Lord, let me not allow this time of worship to become a dead ritual and routine that I follow just because it's the right thing to do. Instead, let me live a life that waits in eager expectation for the opportunity to worship you in spirit and truth. Prepare my heart, O God, to be submitted and surrendered to your will and way so that I will live a fruitful life for your glory alone. In Jesus' name, Amen.

Day 37: Monday's Motivation:

He who dwells in the shelter of the Most High
will abide in the shadow of the Almighty.
I will say to the LORD, "My refuge and my fortress,
my God in whom I trust."—Psalm 91:1-2

Protected With a Promise

Protection, especially in today's chaotic world, is important. Most individuals have an alarm system in their homes. Locked doors and insurance policies are the norm, and children grab their parents' hands when they are afraid or overwhelmed with uncertainty. Even animals seek protection when they feel threatened. We inherently crave protection and security from the things that we believe have the potential to harm us and produce suffering. God's children can run to him when faced with danger and uncertainty. God has not only given us insurance, but he has also promised the assurance of eternal life for those who trust in him (1 John 2:23-25). Fears will come, but run to him and find shelter in him. Daily rely on his presence and protection. He is above all, in all, and over all. There's safety in the arms of God, and in your greatest joys and deepest cries, you are his. That's a promise straight from the Lord.

A Closer Look:

1. Do you think people place too much trust in manmade security measures?

2. Do you believe spiritual protection is more or less important than physical protection?

3. Have there been times when you dismissed the sustainable and promising protection of the Lord?

4. What does it mean for the Lord to protect his children?

Day 38: Tuesday's Treasure:

*But you are a chosen race, a royal priesthood, a holy nation,
a people for his own possession, that you may proclaim
the excellencies of him who called you out of darkness
into his marvelous light.—1 Peter 2:9*

A New Hard Drive

Words spoken can hurt or heal. Children sometimes receive life-altering negative declarations that become self-fulfilling prophecies. Sometimes in the heat of the moment, people say hurtful things that stick. These ideas become embedded, where they play over and over, impacting not only childhood, but flow on through adulthood as well. A computer's hard drive works in the same way, saving data and information until it is changed or deleted. Sometimes files must be deleted in order to prevent an aggravating slowdown of the computer. I remember a time when my computer began to run slower than normal. A friend asked me an important question, "How many unnecessary files are on your computer?" I deleted old files, and over time, my computer functioned normally. Let's examine our own lives. What files have been downloaded on the hard drive of your heart and mind? God speaks in Exodus 19:5-6, and now he speaks through Peter to remind God's people of their identity. We are God's chosen people, called to be in a relationship with Jesus Christ and live in harmony with his word. He has set us free from the darkness of yesterday and has brought us into the newness of today. Allow the Holy Spirit to delete old hurts, broken promises, or unhealthy ideas, freeing up space on your heart's "hard drive" to embrace the new identity Jesus Christ gives to all who trust in him (2 Cor. 5:17).

A Closer Look:

1. Does knowing your identity in Christ change the way you see yourself and your relationships?

2. What are some things in your life that need to be erased so that you can experience freedom?

Day 39: Wednesday's Weapon:

> *So we built the wall. And all the wall was*
> *joined together to half its height, for the*
> *people had a mind to work.—Nehemiah 4:6*

The Right Mind

Opposition is inevitable. Challenges and controversy will show up and force their way in. The critics will arise, the accusers will flourish, and the enemy will aggressively attack; but how should we respond? Our responsibility is to remain focused on God's plan for our lives or risk being distracted by the happenings that surround us. Nehemiah, when faced with opposition, kept his heart and mind in the right place. He maintained the right perspective, the right attitude. He remained focused on God and continued to work. Instead of giving up, running away, and becoming the enemy's instrument of destruction, he continued to build. Don't get so worn out over the present that pressure causes your resolve to cave in and makes you forget your future. Follow Nehemiah's example and depend upon God, despite the opposition. Today, pick up the tools you've laid down, dust yourself off, and get back to work. Those who are capable yet fail to use their God-given gifts are wasting a most precious commodity. This is especially true in the spiritual realm. Christians who have the mind of Christ will be victorious, and God will be glorified (Phil. 2:2-5). He is fighting for you and working in you. Through him you can overcome any obstacle by having a right mind, the mind of Christ.

A Closer Look:

1. Have you ever felt discouraged and defeated? How did you respond?

2. How would you define "perseverance"?

3. In what ways can you demonstrate the character of Nehemiah when it seems as if all odds are against you?

Day 40: Thursday's Truth:

*And he said to all, "If anyone would come after me,
let him deny himself and take up his cross daily
and follow me."—Luke 9:23*

The High Cost

Being a Christian is the call to self-denial, and no one demonstrated that better than Jesus Christ himself. Luke gives us heart-wrenching and soul-stirring words from the Savior. These words are challenging but rewarding, and bold but beautiful. Rather than a huge crowd, Jesus sought a faithful people, those who would be dedicated to his mission and purpose. The self-denial that Jesus calls for means to love him with every fiber of our being, which leads us to willingly obey the commandments of Christ (John 14:15). This relationship calls us to service and divine love for our neighbors; it may also bring about persecution and even dying for his name's sake (Matt. 5:10). This is all too familiar as we watch our local and national news while Christians are dying for their faith. The reality of losing in order to gain and dying to live is pushed aside in our culture, but frequently mentioned through the pages of Scripture. The Gospel is not about pomp and circumstance; it's about daily taking up your cross, denying yourself, and following Jesus. Be willing to lay aside the weights and sins and pursue Christ, withholding nothing (Heb. 12:1-2). Jesus paid the highest cost, giving his life to pay for your sins. Make the decision to repent, embrace his forgiveness, and experience the true joy of being a Christ follower.

A Closer Look:

1. Do you find it difficult to follow Jesus in a world that is constantly fighting for your loyalty and attention?

2. Identify the things and people that are preventing you from wholeheartedly pursuing Christ.

3. What does it mean to be a disciple of Jesus Christ?

Day 41: Friday's Freedom:

> *The LORD is near to all who call on him,*
> *to all who call on him in truth.—Psalm 145:18*

Closer Than You Think

Rejection has touched every life in one way or another. Someone says they will call back; a couple of months pass, and the realization hits that they never called. Or maybe we asked for information via email or text and never received a response. Perhaps there has been a breach in a relationship, a layoff from a job, or a refusal from a place of employment. It can leave us feeling disconnected, lonely, and neglected. Throughout history, especially in America, slave owners mistreated African-Americans, treating them as property and stripping away personal identity and the very humanity to which each person, as a creation of God, is entitled. Faith and trust in God allowed them to stand, knowing that deliverance and freedom would come. Even today, troubling circumstances or problems that can seem devastating and insurmountable to our human senses are present. These experiences can bring us to a place of hopelessness, but lean into Christ, who is near and will never leave us. In this Psalm David gives us hope and assurance. The Lord is near (Ps. 46:1)! What a great promise! When it seems as if Christ is nowhere to be found, remember, he is near. David gives this song of praise to redirect our focus toward intimacy with the Father. The closer you draw to Christ, the more you will experience his peace and presence (James 4:8). He is your source and your sustainer, and he is always closer than our finite minds can possibly comprehend.

A Closer Look:

1. What are some ways you can be intentional about drawing closer to Christ?

2. What does it mean to "call on the Lord in truth?"

Day 42: Saturday's Strength:

> *For you know the grace of our Lord Jesus Christ,*
> *that though he was rich, yet for your sake*
> *he became poor, so that you by his poverty*
> *might become rich.—2 Corinthians 8:9*

True Riches

We are called to be servants of the Lord Jesus Christ. He modeled perfect humility, submission, and obedience to the Father (Phil. 2:7-8). He did not come to please the crowd, but to give his life as a ransom, and our proper response is worship and faithful obedience. Jesus encountered common people who had no material wealth, but he offered something far better than material riches. He willingly sacrificed his life to offer priceless gifts beyond human comprehension, the gifts of salvation, a personal relationship with him, and eternal life. Christ knew and demonstrated suffering for the sake of another in order to ultimately bring glory to the Father. He took the form of man, was falsely accused as a criminal, and suffered to the point of death to set us free from warranted death and punishment. Because of his sacrifice and resurrection, we are made anew to experience a myriad of spiritual blessings (Eph. 1:3-4). Share this good news with others so that they, too, can experience the power of Christ in their lives. At the start of this new day, remember that Christ knows where you are, and he's right there with you. He understands and he desires to speak to you and strengthen you. Christ gave his life so that you could experience the joy and promise of eternal life, the most blessed of all the true riches God bestows upon his children.

A Closer Look:

1. What does it mean that Christ died for the spiritually poor?

2. In response to Christ's dying for the spiritually poor, what is our responsibility as the body of Christ?

Week 7: Days 43~49

Day 43: Sunday's Celebration:

Bless the LORD, O my soul, and all that is within me,
bless his holy name! Bless the Lord, O my soul, and forget not all
his benefits, who forgives all your iniquity, who heals all your
diseases, who redeems your life from the pit, who crowns you
with steadfast love and mercy, who satisfies you with good
so that your youth is renewed like the eagle's.—Psalm 103:1-5

A Reason to Rejoice

There's nothing like a loving Father, one who teaches his children about the gospel of Christ, moreover, one who provides for, supports, and protects them. This is something all people want. However, some may never know what having a loving earthly father is like. Their memories may be colored with darkness and pain, but everyone is invited to experience the love and blessings of the heavenly Father. God loved you so much that he sent his Son into the world to die for you to provide freedom and eternal life (John 3:16-17). Because of Christ's lovingkindness and tender mercies, you can experience forgiveness of your sins, healing from physical and spiritual sickness, and deliverance from the chains of bondage and sin. Jesus Christ is the one who satisfies your every need. Worship and sing praises to God, and walk in forgiveness and thankfulness for the cross of Christ! His sacrificial love and provision are the greatest reasons to rejoice.

A Prayer to Start Your Week

Lord, you are a loving and forgiving Father. You are the healer, provider, redeemer, and sustainer. Words can't describe your greatness and magnificence. Thank you, Lord, for all that you are, and for all that you've done in my life. May I never forget your goodness and mercy, and may I always be sensitive to your voice and never lose sight of your presence. Search me, O God. Cleanse and renew me so that I can walk in everlasting freedom and declare your praises for generations to come. In Jesus' name, Amen.

Day 44: Monday's Motivation:

Remember not the former things,
nor consider the things of old.
Behold, I am doing a new thing; now it springs forth,
do you not perceive it?—Isaiah 43:18-19

Moving Forward

Moving forward is sometimes one of the hardest things to do. Leaving home for a job, getting married, going away for school, or facing tragedy can alter someone's entire life. Whether we feel prepared or not, these decisions can produce a wealth of emotions. As human beings, our complacency and desire for comfort lead us to find peace and satisfaction in the "norm." We embrace our present reality and never believe that life will get better. The Israelites had to be encouraged and reminded of God's promise of deliverance (Isa. 42:6-7). We can become so focused on what's in front of us that what God wants to show us gets cast aside. Jesus' ministry serves as the perfect example of forward movement that all believers should seek to emulate. In the Garden of Gethsemane, Jesus faced a terrible choice, at least in human terms. His human side did not relish the idea of a torturous and lengthy death. Yet, if he had refused to accept his calling, all mankind would have been forever lost without hope (Heb. 9:22). Keep moving forward with your eyes fixed on Jesus. Focusing on the wounds and bruises of the past can blind you to what God wants to do through you. The past is the enemy to the present and future. Allow God to do something brand new to keep you moving forward.

A Closer Look:

1. Have you ever found yourself dwelling on the past? If so, what are some ways you can move forward?

2. Why do you think God wants his people to get beyond the past and look toward the future?

Day 45: Tuesday's Treasure:

*"For the Son of Man came to seek
and to save the lost."—Luke 19:10*

You Matter

All throughout Scripture, every individual who encountered Jesus was transformed. Jesus healed and continues to heal physically, and he also seeks to provide spiritual healing and wholeness. This story in the Gospel of Luke illustrates an encounter Zacchaeus had with Jesus. Zacchaeus had a lot going against him: he was "small of stature," and he was employed as a tax collector who became rich at the expense of common people (Luke 19:2-3). He was known by his occupation and by his relationship with his clients. Zacchaeus was not considered to be one of the "elect," but he did not allow his reputation to get in the way of his pursuit of Christ. Some may see themselves as Zacchaeus did, and as a result, are ready to give up. Several things can prevent us from encountering Jesus: opinions, guilt, and insecurities, which, unfortunately, cause us to give up. Not so fast, my friend! Good news! Christ came JUST for us! He wants to make the rough places smooth and the crooked places straight (Luke 3:5). Jesus came to look for and rescue the lost. We are his treasure, an original portrait that God wants to clean and restore; God himself calls us the apple of his eye (Zech. 2:8). Zacchaeus' humility before Christ was the defining moment in his life. It is in humility and transparency before the Lord that deliverance and wholeness occur. Embrace this truth and remember that you are loved, you are chosen, you are his, and you matter.

A Closer Look:

1. Have you ever lost something valuable? What was your response?

2. What are you doing to be intentional in sharing the Gospel of Christ with the lost?

Day 46: Wednesday's Weapon:

I appeal to you therefore, brothers, by the
mercies of God, to present your bodies as a
living sacrifice, holy and acceptable to God,
which is your spiritual worship.—Romans 12:1

Living Sacrifice

Paul encourages the church to demonstrate their walk by living a sacrificial life before the Lord. One element of Israelite worship in the Old Testament was the sacrifice of an animal for the atonement of sin (Lev. 4:26-35). Although this form of sacrifice was significant and a necessary element of worship, there is no longer a need for the sacrifice of animals because the ultimate and perfect sacrifice was made by the sacrificial Lamb, Jesus Christ! Because of this sacrifice you have an identity in Christ, and therefore you have a responsibility. Offering your life completely to the work of Christ, in loving obedience is an act of worship. Many things can get in the way to disarm you and strip you of Christ's power. Just as God has a plan for your good, the enemy has a strategic plan for your demise, a plan for failure, discouragement, and destruction (1 Peter 5:8). If you're not careful, he will control your life, and you can fall into bondage to sin and the world. Flee from the cultural norms, embrace and submit to God's word, and live a life of worship. Make a decision today to live for the glory of God in loving obedience, purity, and humility by embracing the sacrificial life that Christ demonstrated.

A Closer Look:

1. What are you living for? Who are you living for?

2. What does it mean to live a sacrificial life before the Lord?

3. Have you ever sacrificed something you dearly loved? How did it make you feel?

Day 47: Thursday's Truth:

> *"For where your treasure is,*
> *there your heart will be also."—Matthew 6:21*

Heart Check-up

As I watched the boisterous winds and rushing waters of Hurricane Katrina invade the city of New Orleans and surrounding areas in August 2005, it brought tears to my eyes to see lives shattered, possessions destroyed, and buildings, homes, and churches flooded. As I rested on the sofa watching the news station give live coverage of what seemed to be a living nightmare of one of the worst storms to hit the state of Louisiana, I could not believe it. There were times when I would see those who looked hopeless and helpless, and there were times when people asked, "Where are my loved ones?" Those I watched were not solely concerned about their belongings; they were looking for their families. As years passed, I began to think about the value of life and what sits on the thrones of our hearts. Our culture seems to seek material things almost to the point of worship, rather than on living for the Savior. While material possessions are important, material objects can never fill a void in our lives; only Christ can (1 John 2:16-17). If our hearts are filled with the things of the world, no room is left for what really matters. Search your heart today and ask the Holy Spirit to reveal to you what you value most. Make the decision to allow God's word to provide a heart check-up so you can cease living for the now and start living for the next: eternity.

A Closer Look:

1. Where do you spend most of your money and time?

2. In what ways can you live a life that is fully committed to the cause of Christ?

Day 48: Friday's Freedom:

Draw near to God, and he will draw near to you.—James 4:8

Removing the Barriers

Imagine being crammed in the car on a long road trip with people and luggage, feeling like a hostage, or in a football stadium with just enough room to breathe. Or maybe feeling as if all the voices, dreams, or God's purpose and plans are crowded out, becoming unclear. We often do not experience the presence of God in our lives because a multitude of things bombard us and compete for first place. Everyone pursues something. Maybe it's a job, career, or a person. Our lives can become hard to handle, like a mundane juggling act. The danger of this pursuit is that it can pull our attention in multiple directions, all of them away from a personal relationship with Christ. Instead, every aspect of our lives should line up with God's direction. There is no promise of a life of pleasure and ease, but our God is a loving, generous Father. He will give you endurance as you walk with him. A strong relationship with Jesus means a longing for fellowship and communion with him, increasing your faith. Put the phone aside, talk to him, and follow him to experience the blessed magnitude of this sacred relationship (Ps. 128:1-2). Ask the Holy Spirit for discernment in removing any barriers that will not allow the experience of freedom that is found only in Jesus Christ.

A Closer Look:

1. What are the things or people who are preventing you from drawing close to God?

2. Do you find it easy or difficult to connect with God?

3. Are you being intentional in your pursuit of intimacy with God? If not, what steps can you take to do so?

Day 49: Saturday's Strength:

> *"I have said these things to you,*
> *that in me you may have peace.*
> *In the world you will have tribulation.*
> *But take heart; I have overcome the world."—John 16:33*

Peace for Your Problems

Storms, whether in nature or in life, are inevitable. We have the choice of having joy or burying ourselves in the depths of our present pain and past failures. Joy is not the absence of suffering; it's the presence of God. It is easy to focus on everything that seems wrong with us and lose focus on who Christ is and what he has done for us. True peace and assurance come only when we live through him and in him. Christ overcame the world, and he is the perfect example of perseverance and endurance in the midst of persecution. When facing trials of all kinds or being attacked on every hand, remember that Christ is your anchor in the midst of the storm (Heb. 6:19-20). Go out today, with strength and hope, knowing that although trials are inevitable, Christ won the victory on the cross. Rest in him, knowing that he offers beauty for ashes and peace for problems. The beautiful lyrics of one of the most beloved hymns of all times, "It Is Well With My Soul," are worth remembering:

> When peace, like a river, attendeth my way,
> When sorrows like sea billows roll;
> Whatever my lot, Thou hast taught me to say,
> It is well, it is well with my soul.[10]
> —Horatio G. Spafford

A Closer Look:

1. Can you honestly say that you are living in peace?

2. Do you believe you can have peace outside of a relationship with Christ?

3. How would you describe "peace"?

Week 8: Days 50~56

Day 50: Sunday's Celebration:

> *I will bless the Lord at all times;*
> *his praise shall continually be in my mouth.*
> *My soul makes its boast in the Lord;*
> *let the humble hear and be glad.*—*Psalm 34:1-2.*

A Declaration

Life can be uncertain, with much to worry and complain about, but choosing to worry or worship is an individual choice. What a great invitation and declaration given by David. He invites us to praise the God who is consistent in the midst of the inconsistencies of life. He understands that our praise to God is not predicated upon what happens in our lives, but rather on the character of God. There are times in life where we may feel that there is nothing to be grateful for, but nothing could be further from the truth. Rather than spewing words of discontent, anger, and envy, choose words that will build up and not tear down (Eph. 4:29). Praise God in the midst of pain, and boast in the power and grace of the Lord. Today, let praise become faith-filled and heartfelt. Declaring God's greatness to others will impact, encourage, and lift their lives. As a sacred old hymn, "All Hail the Power of Jesus' Name," proclaims:

> All hail the pow'r of Jesus' Name!
> Let angels prostrate fall;
> Bring forth the royal diadem,
> And crown Him Lord of all![11]
> —Edward Perronet

A Prayer to Start Your Week

> *Lord, life is full of uncertainties, and there are times where I am unsure of my future or your plan for my life, but let me find rest in you and your perfect plan. Let me not become so focused on what I want that I miss your divine will that was set in place from before I was formed in my mother's womb. Lord, I love you, and I praise you. In Jesus' name, Amen.*

Day 51: Monday's Motivation:

For God gave us not a spirit of fear
but of power and love and self-control.—*2 Timothy 1:7*

Fear Not

Fear does not fight fair, and no individual can be truly impactful without overcoming it. Fear causes us to give up in the midst of difficulties and can paralyze all who walk in its ways. As Paul comes to the end of his ministry, he encourages Timothy to endure and persevere, even in the face of possible significant danger. Paul reminds Timothy that God has given him power to endure and stand against the attacks of the evil one. Despite opposition, Timothy is able to go forward in God's grace. Fear and uncertainty occur in life, desiring to stifle and disable us. When anxiety arises, it causes us to lose traction by derailing our emotions and seeking to destroy our souls. But there is an antidote—it's found in Jesus Christ (1 John 4:17-18). He gives us love, power, and self-control. Make the decision to rely on God's might, and remember that Christ came to provide power and love that live inside of you. Today, fearlessly walk in boldness and in the grace of our Lord and Savior Jesus Christ.

A Closer Look:

1. Identify some of your fears. Why are you fearful concerning these things?

2. What does it mean to endure and persevere even when circumstances might tempt you to worry?

3. How can you be more intentional in walking with God on a daily basis?

Day 52: Tuesday's Treasure:

And whatever you do, in word or deed,
do everything in the name of the Lord Jesus,
giving thanks to God the Father
through him.—Colossians 3:17

Living for Christ

We all love to be acknowledged and appreciated, both personally and professionally. Accolades or trophies are welcome tributes, but in all honesty, hearing the applause and cheers from the crowd can lead us to believe that our own efforts make us special. It's fine to celebrate the milestones and monumental moments of life, and there's joy in honoring others. However, success and accomplishments can get the best of us without vigilant resistance to an elevated sense of self (Rom. 12:3). While working as unto the Lord is a calling that should instill pride in all we do, as Christ followers, we live to further his kingdom and name. Our relationship with Christ compels us to make a difference in the lives of others. Living in contradistinction to a world that is self-centered and confused about what it means to unwaveringly follow Christ can be difficult, but the Lord never promised it would be easy (John 16:32-33). One of the most powerful gestures you can make is demonstrating Jesus through acts of kindness. Living for Christ is possible only when you have surrendered your life to his rule and reign as Lord and Savior. When your life becomes synonymous with Christ's will, lives are influenced by your example, making an eternal impact upon the world.

A Closer Look:

1. What do you believe God's purpose is for your life?

2. What does it mean to be God's representative and ambassador in the earth?

3. How do your actions and good deeds bring glory to God?

Day 53: Wednesday's Weapon:

And the angel of the LORD appeared
to him and said to him, "The LORD is with you,
O mighty man of valor."—Judges 6:12

Chosen

Like Gideon, there are times in life when we feel undeserving or ill-equipped to be strong servants and representatives of God. We become distracted by our past, disturbed by the present, and blinded to the future. These conditions could lead to weaknesses and insecurities, causing us to question whether God is really there. Someone may be looking for love in the wrong places and from the wrong people, but God has given us a new identity, and it is found in Jesus Christ, the one who loved us from the beginning (Eph. 1:4-5). Flee from falling into discouragement and apathy. The enemy wants us to give up and lose hope in the Savior, but let us rest in Jesus, knowing that he has us in the palms of his hands. He loves us; he has a plan for our lives. No matter where you have come from, you can be used by God. Gideon felt outnumbered and insignificant, but God saw it differently. God used Gideon to lead his people to victory and was faithfully with him, and God will lead you, too. Although honorable, being chosen by people for events, honors, or any number of other things pales in comparison to being chosen by God. In fact, there is no comparison. Stand in faith and rest assured that just as God was with Gideon, he has chosen you and will remain with you.

A Closer Look:

1. Have you ever felt unqualified or unequipped to do what God called you to do?

2. When you look in the mirror, what comes to mind?

3. Have you ever been chosen last as a team member, or perhaps not chosen for an assignment you really wanted and felt you deserved? Does this help you to fully realize just how special being chosen by God is?

Day 54: Thursday's Truth:

> *But Daniel resolved that he would not defile himself*
> *with the king's food, or with the wine that he drank.*
> *Therefore he asked the chief of the eunuchs*
> *to allow him not to defile himself.*—Daniel 1:8

Take a Stand

Daniel was decidedly counter-cultural during his lifetime. This young man refused to taint himself by taking food and drink that belonged to idols. Daniel was so committed to God that he did not want anything to stain his witness and calling. What a great example. Society offers endless enticements, and it can be all too easy to give in to them. Temptation is knocking, but we do not have to answer. The choice is ours. Even if it means standing alone, God enables us to stand firm. The Lord stood alone for all mankind; he hung alone on the cross he bore. He died alone for the atonement of our sins; he alone took the punishment that we deserved (1 Peter 2:24). He did all these things alone on our behalf, not only to spare us from experiencing the torture and death he endured, but also because he loved us so much he wanted to give us a way to be in relationship with him now and throughout eternity. The Lord blessed Daniel because he could be trusted. What if God is not calling you to find comfort in our culture, but to stand as Daniel did and live by a standard that glorifies the Lord? Today, make the decision not to allow anything or anyone to taint the witness you are for Christ. The moment you comply with culture, that's the moment your fervor is lost. Today, turn away from the corruption of this world, and take a stand.

A Closer Look:

1. As you examine your life, do you live to fit in or stand out?

2. What are some ways you can remain Godly in an ungodly world?

Day 55: Friday's Freedom:

Do not be conformed to this world, but be transformed
by the renewal of your mind, that by testing
you may discern what is the will of God,
what is good and acceptable and perfect.—Romans 12:2

Stand Out

There's a constant battle that goes on between our two ears and for some, it is the devil's workshop. A perverted mind will eventually lead one to live a perverted life. Paul warns the church at Rome to not conform to the patterns of the world or present age. When one subscribes to such a lifestyle, it leads down the road of death, destruction, and disaster. There are various ways to stand out. Compare today's headlines and the lives of high-profile people with the Godly people described in God's word. While entertainers, politicians, and other well-known personalities stand out, it is often for reasons that are vile or offensive. As Christians, we must stand out for the right reasons, to glorify God. Living a transformed life from the inside out must first take place in our minds as we submit to the leading of the Holy Spirit. When God's word is your focus, your life will be guarded and guided by the word. Through God's word, his will for your life is abundantly clear. If life seems like one big whirlwind, start feeding on God's word. Hiding this precious knowledge deep in your heart builds up your resolve not to be moved by feelings, but rather, to know Christ and his call and purpose for your life (Ps. 119:10-16).

A Closer Look:

1. Do you believe it is easier to conform to the environment around you or transform the environment around you?

2. What are some ways you are being intentional about living a life that is not reflective of the culture around you?

Day 56: Saturday's Strength:

Fear not, for I am with you; be not dismayed,
for I am your God; I will strengthen you,
I will help you, I will uphold you with
my righteous right hand.—Isaiah 41:10

Trustworthy

Nothing hurts worse than broken promises. Words can fall to the ground and shatter before our very eyes, leaving our lives fragmented, hopeless, and helpless. This is the unspoken issue that plagues many individuals. Neglect and betrayal as a result of what has happened to us can become our constant companions. Unfortunately, these experiences can cause us to blame God and fall victim to the deception that God can't be trusted. Having distorted beliefs about God is the very thing that keeps us from truly experiencing his presence and power in our lives. We must hold fast to the promises of God. Remember that God is for you; don't allow disappointment to grow and create discontent. He will strengthen you and defend you, so trust God's promise in the midst of your present predicament (Ps. 37:17). As God promised to restore Israel, he will keep his promises to you as well. He will help you to overcome obstacles and will lead you to the straight paths, restoring your peace and joy, and ensuring your victory in him. Because he is trustworthy, his precious promises are priceless truths.

A Closer Look:

1. How do you feel when someone has broken a promise?

2. How does it feel to know that the promises of God will never go unfulfilled?

3. Do the promises of God encourage you to continue to move forward?

Week 9: Days 57~63

Day 57: Sunday's Celebration:

Enter his gates with thanksgiving, and his courts with praise!
Give thanks to him; bless his name!—Psalm 100:4

Heart of Expectation

I remember pep rallies during football season at my high school. The purpose of a pep rally was to generate excitement for the upcoming football game. What would amaze me so much about this event was the amount of energy, enthusiasm, and expectation that would fill the gym. Students would yell, "Go Bears!" In our eagerness to win, the entire gym would shake with hundreds of voices in one accord. This Psalm invites us to reflect upon the mindset that is needed as we enter the house of God, and it instructs us to enter the gates and courts of God's house with thankful hearts and praise. There was so much about my high school's football team that students could have pinpointed to complain about, but it was more exciting to celebrate and gather expectantly instead. As we enter into the house of worship today, there are choices to make: we can complain, or we can have an attitude of expectation (Ps. 86:12-13). Choose to be hopeful while waiting with anticipation. Offer him praises because life could be worse. The Lord has given you just enough strength in the midst of your weakness. Get excited about worship, and celebrate the small victories with gratitude and thanksgiving. Expect great things and give him praise.

A Prayer to Start Your Week

Lord, I enter your gates with praise and adoration for who you are and all that you've done in and through your people. Help me not to become so consumed with my needs that I forget your wonder and majesty. Lord, I ask for forgiveness for the times I was self-centered. Help me to remember that with you all things are possible, so I can expect miracles in my life and in the lives of others. I want to make your name great in all the earth, from now until eternity. In Jesus' name, Amen.

Day 58: Monday's Motivation:

Brothers, I do not consider that I have made it my own.
But one thing I do: forgetting what lies behind
and straining forward to what lies ahead.
I press on toward the goal for the prize
of the upward call of God in Christ Jesus.—Philippians 3:13-14

An Eternal Focus

Building an identity based on the past is not only a poor choice, but also a waste of what could be. This mindset is tragic, causing us to take on the identity of our struggles and failing to realize the blind spots that exist. Paul had to make the decision to forget the past and move toward Christ-likeness with an eternal perspective. Living in the past will ultimately destroy our lives; instead, push past the pain and learn from it. While some setbacks are by choice, some are unwarranted. However, no matter how they arrive, this horrible pit is no place to reside. Clinging to the past blocks the blessings of the future. The only thing from the past that has any real meaning is what Jesus did for us on the cross. Any past disturbing earthly events, hurtful circumstances, or mistakes in our own lives should be laid at the foot of the cross and left there (Matt. 11:28-30). Let go of yesterday in order to embrace today, and live with eternity in view. As sinners saved by grace, we have a blessed reason to rejoice (Eph. 2:8-9). We have been redeemed! Leaving the past behind allows us to maintain an eternal focus.

A Closer Look:

1. Do you become so focused on the past or present that you lose sight of the future?

2. What are some ways you can live with an eternal perspective?

Day 59: Tuesday's Treasure:

"You are the salt of the earth,
but if salt has lost its taste,
how shall its saltiness be restored?
It is no longer good for anything except to be thrown out
and trampled under people's feet."—Matthew 5:13

Stay Salty

There's nothing like a pinch of salt sprinkled to enhance the quality of food and make it more enjoyable. But God's word gives salt a spiritual connotation, too. As Jesus sat preaching, he taught that his followers have a calling: to be the salt of the earth. We are called to enhance the places where God sends us by reflecting the image of Christ in the earth in both word and deed. Blending in with the world dilutes our effectiveness in the kingdom of God. Christians were never intended to blend in. The very purpose of our lives as followers of Christ is to be "different" and to demonstrate his love to the lost (1 Peter 1:13-16). Keep him high and lifted up to allow the true salt of the earth to flavor the lives of all who will simply believe in him, ask for his forgiveness, and live for him. Today, sprinkle some salt here and there and make a difference. Sprinkle words of kindness and encouragement on someone who is hurting. Invest time and effort to preserve a relationship and to be there for a friend. Live the Gospel and share it for his glory. Your efforts to promote God's message and live for him ensure that you stay salty.

A Closer Look:

1. Have you ever felt out of place at a social gathering or event? Describe your experience.

2. As you live your life as a Christ follower, are you aware that you will never fit in with a world that has lost its flavor and saltiness? How does that make you feel?

Day 60: Wednesday's Weapon:

> *Put on the whole armor of God,*
> *that you may be able to stand against*
> *the schemes of the devil.—Ephesians 6:11*

Suited for Battle

Every morning, we shower, brush our teeth, comb our hair, and make sure we have our cell phones. We prepare externally, but if we fail to prepare internally, our guard is down. The Christian walk is one that requires us to know our adversary; Satan is real. One of the most naïve mindsets we can have is to believe that the devil is not at work seeking to destroy, accuse, and bring about our demise each and every day (1 Peter 5:8). Be aware, but do not be afraid. The only way to stand against the works and plans of the devil is by learning how to fight. Christ has won the victory, but that doesn't mean that the devil has tucked his tail. Fight by standing in harmony with God's word. When feelings of being attacked occur, stay in God's word, pray, and sing praises to him; these are the weapons God provides for defense (2 Cor. 10:3). This preparation ensures that the enemy's attacks will not be successful; you can stand firm and be victorious. The enemy is wily in his schemes and approaches, but God's armor, protection, and wisdom through his precious word will always prevail. A line from the movie, *War Room,* states a wise truth, "To win the fight, you've got to have the right resources, because victories don't come by accident."[12] Suit up daily and prepare for battle, assured that with God's armor, victory is certain.

A Closer Look:

1. What are your thoughts about spiritual warfare, and how do you respond when attacked spiritually?

2. Read Ephesians 6:10-18. As you consider each piece of the armor of God, in what ways do you think the armor protects you?

3. When you think about battles, what comes to mind?

Day 61: Thursday's Truth:

*"Then you will call upon me and come and pray to me,
and I will hear you. You will seek me and find me
when you seek me with all your heart."— Jeremiah 29:12-13*

God in the Midst

When I was growing up, kids at school would make a "pinkie promise." This promise would solidify and make certain that what was spoken would not leave the mouth of the individual who heard it. Within our culture and world, promises are made without deep thought or reflection, giving us false promises and little hope. Our human minds tend to focus on life's conflicts or difficulties. However, in the midst of exile and tumultuous times, God spoke through his mouthpiece, Jeremiah, to remind his people that he is trustworthy. Remain faithful to call on him and seek him fervently through prayer, knowing that God is faithful and always present. That's great news! The sun may be shining, or the dark clouds may be hovering overhead, causing uncertainty. Remember, you can count on the Lord's promises. God is not only in the midst, he is also over all. He has the vantage point of heaven as his perspective. This viewpoint means that life's trials are minute compared to the greatness of our God. Seek him, call on him, and trust him. He hears your cries, and he is close to the brokenhearted (Ps. 34:17-18). Regardless of the difficulties that come your way, you can be certain that God is in the midst, and he is in control.

A Closer Look:

1. Have you been in a place of hopelessness? Take time to write down your experience.

2. With today's Scripture from Jeremiah in your heart and mind, in what ways can your hope and strength be renewed?

Day 62: Friday's Freedom:

*Jesus said to her, "I am the resurrection and the life.
Whoever believes in me, though he die,
yet shall he live."—John 11:25*

Life

When all hope seems lost, Christ can surprise us with amazing circumstances that radically change our lives. Any circumstance produces two options: either run to Christ, or run from Christ, blaming others. In this story in the Gospel of John, it seems as if Christ has forgotten about Lazarus, the one he loves. Yet even death did not have the last word. Through Jesus' resurrection power, Lazarus was restored. Life can be harsh; we may find ourselves knocked to our knees, asking, "Why?" Whether dealing with a sudden health decline or marital problem, or a disheartening situation in life, we must know that Jesus gives us hope and he responds. We have all had our backs against the wall where things seemed to be dead or lying dormant; however, these moments can become defining moments. Martha experienced such a moment as she responded to Jesus' "tardiness." Her human eyes "saw" that it was too late. Jesus knew that it was only the beginning. We, too, have unexpected challenges where we feel that God has forgotten or is late in responding. As Jesus challenged these two sisters, Mary and Martha, he is challenging you to realize there are no boundaries in an infinite God. Though you may find yourself helpless today, the Creator of life and liberty is the most powerful force and faithful friend that you can count on. Embrace the freedom that he offers, and live for him (Ps. 147:5-6). Christ is the only one who can give and resurrect life.

A Closer Look:

1. What are some areas in your life that seem to be dead or lying dormant?

2. How has Christ been at work in your life in these dying and dormant places?

Day 63: Saturday's Strength:

> *Then he said to me, "This is the word*
> *of the LORD to Zerubbabel:*
> *'Not by might, nor by power, but by my Spirit'*
> *says the LORD of hosts."*—*Zechariah 4:6*

Never Alone

People are commonly told to follow their hearts and that they can become whatever they want to be, whether at home, at school, or in the media. Society communicates these words to emphasize that our futures are in our hands. These words comfort us, giving us hope and permission to live a self-satisfying life. Social conditioning is hypnotic, luring us to live for selfish desires rather than for a purpose that is greater than ourselves. Think about how limited our efforts are without the power of the Holy Spirit. When Christ is at the forefront of our lives, he will be glorified. Money, status, or our abilities alone are unable to fulfill the purposes of our lives; we need the presence of the Holy Spirit as our guide and comforter (John 14:26). Remember that human power alone is insufficient, so earnestly seek God to become more dependent upon him. Without Christ, we are like a car that has an engine, but no gas. No matter how good the engine may be, without gas the destination is unreachable. Embrace this gift that is found only through a personal relationship with Jesus Christ, who will always be there. Life without the Spirit of God is empty, but with the Lord, his guidance and protection assure you that you are never alone.

A Closer Look:

1. Is there anything you are trying to accomplish on your own?

2. Do you find it hard to turn your life and desires over to the Lord?

3. What are some practical ways you can begin to give your desires over to God?

Week 10: Days 64~70

Day 64: Sunday's Celebration:

Great is the LORD, and greatly to be praised,
and his greatness is unsearchable.—Psalm 145:3

Unexplainable Words

There are things in all of our lives that leave us speechless and in awe. I remember visiting Hawaii, and as my wife and I toured the island, we were in awe while standing in the clear, crystal blue water on the oceanfront and driving through the mountains that rest symmetrically along the island. This was God's greatness right before our eyes. All of us ascribe greatness to something or someone in our lives that has impacted and influenced us. This greatness is not necessarily tied to what they've accomplished, but to whom they are. Placing the word "great" in front of these particular people, places, or situations magnifies them to a point beyond their capacity. As David defines greatness, the difference between God's greatness and the greatness ascribed to things or people is that it is *unsearchable,* meaning it cannot be explained or defined. Today, worship the Lord for his greatness. He is our King, our Redeemer, our Savior, and our Creator. The one who set the sun, moon, and stars in place is standing at the door of our hearts, knocking (Ps. 104:19). Rather than trying to explain the unexplainable, let him in today.

A Prayer to Start Your Week

Lord, how wonderful and majestic is your name in all the earth. The mountains bow down, and the earth trembles at the sound of your voice. I stand in awe of your power and greatness, and let me never forget your love, grace, and mercy, and your authority that rules and reigns, now and forever. In Jesus' name, Amen.

Day 65: Monday's Motivation:

> *The LORD is my shepherd; I shall not want.*
> *He makes me lie down in green pastures.*
> *He leads me beside still waters.——Psalm 23:1-2*

The One Who Guides

There's nothing like the protection and guidance of loving parents, especially those who ultimately lead and model how to live according to God's word. Because of our parents' loving guidance and discipline, such a relationship builds trust, and children crave this guidance and love. For some, it may not be a parent, but a teacher or coach. Ultimately, we have put our trust in the hands of someone. Sadly, some children today have never known the love and guidance of a parent who wants to protect and shepherd them. Countless children get lost in the shuffle, in danger of being lost forever, relationally and spiritually, unless Christians around them notice and intervene. Undoubtedly, David has complete trust and dependency in the Lord as his shepherd, to guide, direct, protect, and correct. The shepherd knows his sheep, and the sheep know the shepherd's voice and obey (John 10:14). David finds rest and peace in following the Lord. There is a confidence in David's declaration of who the Lord is in his life. Your loving heavenly Father will lead you like no other. Against the wolves of this world, Jesus shepherds you, and he guides and protects you. Allow the Good Shepherd to lead, and then experience streams of peace and rest where the sweet presence of the Holy Spirit is incomparable.

A Closer Look:

1. List some characteristics of a shepherd. Which of these qualities do you find personally challenging?

2. Read John chapter 10. What does it mean for the Lord to be your Shepherd?

3. Do you find it challenging to trust and follow the Lord during difficult seasons?

Day 66: Tuesday's Treasure:

> *And I will give you a new heart,*
> *and a new spirit I will put within you.*
> *And I will remove the heart of stone from your flesh*
> *and give you a heart of flesh.*——*Ezekiel 36:26*

Out With the Old, In With the New!

The latest gadgets or products always bring a lot of "buzz." For months before the holiday season, commercials and sales flash across our television and computer screens as stores across the country seek to lure buyers for the next "hot" item. Seasonal sales have become year-round marketing deluges. Christmas decorations and gifts appear in October. Chocolates and cards with hearts for Valentine's Day are displayed the day after Christmas. Some holiday seasons overlap, with Easter goodies available along with Valentine's Day items. These items do not come with the disclaimer that their purchase will not bring peace or satisfaction. Things of the flesh cannot bring ultimate peace, but life in the Spirit is what changes us from the inside out (Gal. 3:8). This new heart is a new beginning, a new way of living. Today, accept this gift and live in a manner which not only reflects his image, but also demonstrates a life under the sovereign rule of God. Surrendering your life over to Christ brings about a transformed heart and a renewed mind. Unlike new gadgets and material goods, this willingness to transform your heart and mind does come with a guarantee. You have God's assurance that this is the path to becoming the person God destined you to be.

A Closer Look:

1. Do you find yourself easily angered and feeling as if no one cares about you?

2. What does it mean for Christ to give you a new heart and spirit? How would that change your life?

Day 67: Wednesday's Weapon:

*And the peace of God, which surpasses
all understanding, will guard your hearts and
your minds in Christ Jesus.*——*Philippians 4:7*

Rest

In this day and age, life has a way of meeting us at the front door with demands, responsibilities, and deadlines, some of which can become overwhelming. Sometimes it feels as though life is on a downward spiral. We may have bought clothes or the newest electronic gadget, gotten married, moved to the ideal city, and possibly received our dream job, but it can still seem as if something is missing. We get caught up in the hustle and bustle of work, taking children to sports practice, or scurrying off to take care of some task. Life can become so "busy" that even church has to be "fit in" at times, even though coming to the Lord's house to worship him should be a primary source of joy, rather than a burden. Spiritually, our hands are tied behind our backs, leaving us stranded in the middle of the sea of life without a lifejacket or paddle, and the winds and waves are tossing vehemently. In the midst of life's circumstances and unanswered questions, Paul gives the key that will change the trajectory of our lives. To withstand the turbulence of life, embrace the peace that comes only from Jesus Christ. This peace is experienced in your heart and mind, but it affects every aspect of your life. It will protect you and watch over you when embraced (Col. 3:15). Ask the Lord for his peace, and then simply rest.

A Closer Look:

1. Do you ever ask the question, "Why me?"
2. How are you trusting God in those "why me" moments?

Day 68: Thursday's Truth:

> *If any of you lacks wisdom, let him ask God,*
> *who gives generously to all without reproach,*
> *and it will be given him.—James 1:5*

Looking For Wisdom?

Have you ever heard that knowledge is power, or that increased knowledge will better prepare you to take the world by storm? The problem with this approach is that when knowledge is mistaken for wisdom, the facts are simply manipulated in an effort to make good choices and decisions. Facts can prove to be untrue because human beings are providing the facts, possibly making the facts inherently flawed. Science presents theories, hoping to prove them as facts, but many people blindly accept scientific theories as truth. While it's important to pursue knowledge and understanding, it cannot be divorced from wisdom. We must grow in both minds and hearts. Knowledge is knowing "how" to do, but wisdom is knowing "when" to do by waiting and discerning the will of God as we carefully move forward. As a follower of Christ, wisdom calls for you to move from just hearing God's word to living it out. Wisdom is available to all, and the Lord is faithful to grant the gift of wisdom when you ask him (1 Kings 3:9). Today, make the choices that will glorify him, and live a life that will make an eternal difference.

A Closer Look:

1. What areas of your life do you feel need work in living a life that embodies wisdom?

2. Identify some individuals in your life who display wisdom in their lives and the decisions they make. In what ways are these people unique?

Day 69: Friday's Freedom:

So Jesus said to the Jews who had believed him, "If you abide in my word, you are truly my disciples."—John 8:31

Stay Rooted

Whatever has our attention reveals what is most important to us. The music we listen to, our conversations with others, and the shows we watch say a lot about our character and maturity. Ask the Holy Spirit for guidance in these areas. For some, Jesus is a part of their lives, but here's the heart-wrenching question: is he at the center? It's important to challenge our thinking. Are we moved by feelings, or by God's word? Ponder these questions, and examine the answers carefully. Every day, being fed spiritually is just as important as consuming food for our bodies. Make God's word and your relationship with him priorities. True disciples of Jesus Christ not only talk the talk, but they also walk the walk. Begin today by living out his word, but the first step is taking time to read his word, asking God for discernment through prayer. Let today be the beginning of a journey toward the desire to stay planted in God's word. Submission to these Spirit-breathed words confronts, convicts, and calls you to higher heights and deeper depths in your relationship with Christ (2 Tim. 3:16-17). Living in this way, instead of being swayed by society, you will develop deep spiritual roots and be strengthened by the Savior.

A Closer Look:

1. What does it mean to abide in Christ?

2. Do you believe it is important to live a fruitful life?

3. What kind of fruit is evident in your life?

Day 70: Saturday's Strength:

> *Not that I am speaking of being in need, for*
> *I have learned in whatever situation I am to be content.*
> *I know how to be brought low, and I know how to abound.*
> *In any and every circumstance, I have learned*
> *the secret of facing plenty and hunger, abundance*
> *and need. I can do all things through him*
> *who strengthens me.—Philippians 4:11-13*

How Do You See It?

Is life satisfying, or do complaints take center stage? Maybe your focus is on everything that seems wrong with your life, and it sidetracks you through missed opportunities, broken promises, or present pains and struggles. Instead of throwing in the towel and falling into a place of cynicism, realize that Jesus Christ is for you. Know that all of your experiences can either propel you toward Christ or detour you. Paul experienced tumultuous times in life, but instead of complaining and becoming bitter, he learned contentment (2 Cor. 11:24-31). The Apostle Paul can teach all of us a fresh perspective. Don't allow the current state to limit, but allow it to propel and strengthen. The pressure of life's currents remind us that only through Christ can we withstand the difficulties of life. So, regardless of how things look, you can bring glory to the Savior by being content and waiting to see what he wants to show you. Examining the way you see things and being willing to change your perspective allow you to see Christ at work in the highs and lows.

A Closer Look:

1. Identify those areas of discontent in your life. Pray daily for God's help.

2. What does it mean to be content?

3. If difficult circumstances occur, can you still be content?

Week 11: Days 71~77

Day 71: Sunday's Celebration:

Praise the LORD! Sing to the LORD a new song, his praise in the assembly of the godly! Let Israel be glad in his Maker; let the children of Zion rejoice in their King!—Psalm 149:1-2

Like-minded Worship

There's nothing like the energy and unity that fill a space when everyone is of one accord. People who join together with like-minded purpose and passion create an effective movement. When the body of Christ gathers with the purpose of glorifying God, they unite in praise with one voice. Praise and worship are music to the Lord's ears because he longs for the praises of those he loves so dearly and for whom he has freely given so much. Having a united purpose will encourage and challenge us as we come to worship the King of kings. Let us come not only to receive, but also to give. Rejoice in whom God is: your maker, motivator, and the epitome of mercy, the King whose kingdom has no end. When you have this perspective, healing for your soul and transformation in your mind takes place. Enter worship today with like-minded focus. Worship and rejoice in the King of kings and the Lord of lords, Jesus Christ!

A Prayer to Start Your Week

Lord, you are my Creator. Before I was formed in my mother's womb, you knew me, and had my purpose and destiny set in place. Let me not become so discouraged by life that your will becomes foggy and non-existent. I desire to worship and praise you because you are my God and King, the one who rules and reigns with all power and dominion. In Jesus' name, Amen.

Day 72: Monday's Motivation:

Trust in the LORD with all your heart,
and do not lean on your own understanding,
in all your ways acknowledge him,
and he will make straight your paths.—*Proverbs 3:5-6*

I Don't Understand

There are some occurrences in life that are beyond our understanding. Some come in the form of tragedy, sickness, and betrayal. Everyone would like an explanation for life's happenings, and we are taught to seek understanding in all things. Without this pursuit, a sense of being lost envelops us, but first we must seek faith to have understanding. The world's viewpoint teaches that true success is in how much we know and own, but the truth is that our finite minds simply cannot fathom the mysteries behind God's ways (Isa. 55:8-9). Perhaps the path is winding through a dark season and there's no light in view, but trust in Christ, the one who holds all things together (Col. 1:17). It's important to seek understanding, but ask God to inspire the wisdom to trust him despite the reality. Yes, it can be difficult, but we weren't created to wallow in the pits of despair, feeling hopeless. Trust in his word. He has us in the palms of his hands. God desires our faith, the faith that trusts God when it seems illogical or incomprehensible. There's beauty in trusting in the Lord, the one who is sovereign, merciful, and gracious. You don't have to understand the "why" of a situation. The important thing is to understand and trust in the faithfulness of God, and to know that he is in control.

A Closer Look:

1. What does it mean to trust?

2. Are there areas in your life where you feel you need more understanding regarding God's will and purpose in your life?

3. Are you willing to use God's word as the basis for making a plan to gain greater understanding?

Day 73: Tuesday's Treasure:

> *Love is patient and kind; love does not envy or boast;*
> *it is not arrogant or rude. It does not insist on its own way;*
> *it is not irritable or resentful;*
> *it does not rejoice at wrongdoing,*
> *but rejoices with the truth.*
> *Love bears all things, believes all things,*
> *hopes all things, endures all things.—1 Corinthians 13:4-7*

Love at Its Best

One of the hardest things in life is to love those who seem unlovable. Love is the foundation of any and every Godly relationship. However, without knowing that we are loved by the Father, it is difficult to express and embrace love's beauty. Moreover, without the love of God expressed through Christ, we would be hopeless, without purpose and lacking the ability to love our neighbor. When love steps into the ring, it challenges our motives and our understanding. It demands our attention and time and requires us to lay aside our pride. True love never loses the fight. If our love for Christ and our fellow brothers or sisters is not the motivating factor for what we do, then our labor is in vain (1 Cor. 13:1-3). Love is the complete opposite of tolerance; it's a standard, a submission to surrender our will to the will of the Father. Love is action, it calls for a response (John 14:15). Because of the Father's great love and mercy, he sent the epitome of love, Jesus Christ, to exemplify that love to the point of death. This love rises, and calls us to surrender. With him, love at its best is possible, but without him it is unreachable.

A Closer Look:

1. Do you find it difficult to love others? Have you asked the Lord for understanding and help in being more loving?

2. Have you studied God's word to learn about the love of Christ? Are you willing to ask God to help you emulate this kind of Christ-like love?

Day 74: Wednesday's Weapon:

> *For she said, "If I touch even his garments,*
> *I will be made well."*—Mark 5:28

One Touch

We can talk ourselves into believing something is true and that life will never change. Often, the rhythm and rhyme of our lives is one sad song after another. The cadence never changes and it becomes frustrating and unbearable. However, the miracle comes in our lives when we choose not to give up, but to embrace the one who has the power to set us free, Jesus Christ. The power and freedom come not in what others say to us, but in what we say to ourselves. The text in the Gospel of Mark introduces a woman who had a sickness for twelve miserable and catastrophic years, full of pain, rejection, and fear. She was seen as a poor, helpless outcast, one whose identity was wrapped in her issue. The only hope for her dilemma was to get to Jesus. In Mark 5:27 she heard the reports about Jesus, and desperate for a healing touch, she responded in faith. Maybe you've been struggling for years with a particular physical or emotional issue, making it your new normal. When you are desperate for healing from the Great Physician, you will encounter his supernatural power. Today, press in, reach out, and touch him. There's nothing in your life that Jesus can't free you from. Trust him today. Through just one touch, there's healing for sickness in both body and soul.

A Closer Look:

1. Do you have things in your life, whether physical, emotional, financial, or spiritual, that need healing?

2. Do you need to forgive anyone? Do you need to forgive yourself?

3. What steps can you take in order to draw close to Christ? Is there anything keeping you from intimately pursuing Christ?

Day 75: Thursday's Truth:

You make known to me the path of life;
in your presence there is fullness of joy;
at your right hand are pleasures forevermore. —Psalm 16:11

Stay Close to the Fire

Growing up, I enjoyed watching my father start the fireplace. He would gather wood from beside the house and begin the process of getting the fire started. Some of my best memories are of days when, although it was cold outside, there was a place to go and get warm. I would get as close as possible because the presence of the heat repelled the cold, brisk weather. The closer I got to the warmth, the better I felt. The cold was no longer an issue. Cold and wet days will come. We may be unable to move; things might be uncomfortable, and life might threaten to be one big snow storm, leaving us immobile. Draw near to God, not for the sake of deliverance alone, but for the sake of closeness with our Creator. It is in our closeness that deliverance will come. God's presence is a consuming fire (Heb. 12:28-29). Even the finest gold is put through extreme heat in order to be purified. God's fire not only keeps his power stirred up within your soul, but it also purifies your heart and mind. Pursue an intimate relationship with Christ. Draw close to him; allow the Holy Spirit to burn away those things contrary to his will. Be revived and renewed by staying close to the fire.

A Closer Look:

1. Have you ever experienced the presence of God? Describe how you were changed.

2. Do you find it challenging to pursue intimacy with Christ?

Day 76: Friday's Freedom:

When Jesus saw him lying there and knew that he
had already been there a long time, he said to him,
"Do you want to be healed?"—John 5:6

Get Up

Blaming others for our present circumstance is wasted effort because it will never improve the situation. By doing this, we hope to remove the pressure being focused on us and transfer ownership of that pressure to the situation or person that appears to be the problem. Taking ownership of the problem is the first step toward freedom. Then we must repent, surrender to God, and be forgiving toward others. This is no easy task! Excuses will prevent us from experiencing the freedom that is found in Christ. As the invalid's story in the Gospel of John depicts, this man had been sick for 38 years and had been lying in this state for a very long time. He watched others come and go, passing him by as he wallowed in self-pity and doubt. Jesus showed up, picked him out of the crowd, and asked him this challenging question, "Do you want to be healed?" For many of us, productivity has been put on pause because of what has happened to us. Christ is standing at the pool. He has picked you out and he's asking you the same question. Healing will come when you recognize the source of all healing. Break away from the invalid, lame, and paralyzed mentality, and embrace freedom in the one who conquered death, hell, and the grave. Today, he's standing at the door of your heart, so allow him in, rise up, and walk.

A Closer Look:

1. Do you find it easier to make excuses than to accept responsibility and take action? In your experience, did excuses help or hinder you?

2. What do you think would happen if you removed the excuses and obeyed Christ?

Day 77: Saturday's Strength:

The steadfast love of the LORD never ceases;
his mercies never come to an end;
they are new every morning;
great is your faithfulness.—Lamentations 3:22-23

Faithfulness of God

As part of the human condition, there have been times when we deserved to be punished but were given another chance; we were acquitted (Rom. 5:8-11). Such moments should spark gratitude to God for his unfailing grace and mercy. His love and mercy do not give us permission to play Russian roulette and gamble with our lives to test his patience and lovingkindness. Rather, it should bring us to our knees in thanksgiving and submission to the gracious love, compassion, and faithfulness of our God. His faithful forgiveness is also a reminder to be just as quick to forgive others when we feel we have been treated unfairly, gossiped about, falsely accused, or otherwise treated in ways we feel we do not deserve. Remember God's command to love your enemies, just as he loved you before you ever realized your need for him (Matt. 5:44). Likewise, when you experience undeserved punishment, God's faithfulness and mercy is extended on your behalf. Rest in the one who keeps his promises and whose faithfulness never ceases (Deut. 7:9). Each new sunrise is an opportunity to give thanks to the Lord for his love and faithfulness that will never give up or run out. No matter how hard life seems, reflect back to discover that God's unfailing love and mercy never end because his faithfulness endures forever.

A Closer Look:

1. Think about your life and how far you've come. Do you express gratitude to God for the blessings in your life?

2. Make a list of things you are thankful for. Spend time thanking and praising God for his faithfulness.

Week 12: Days 78~84

Day 78: Sunday's Celebration:

*Sing to him a new song; play skillfully on the strings,
with loud shouts. For the word of the LORD is upright,
and all his work is done in faithfulness.—Psalm 33:3-4*

The Beauty of Worship

There is something special and unique about music.
Whether played at the coronation of kings and queens, or
during the triumphal procession of the inauguration of an
elected official, music is a powerful tool that, when placed in the
proper hands, can set an atmosphere. Music can make a dreary
day glad or can turn a happy mood into a sad, somber feeling.
Some music has the power to draw one closer to God, or it can
cause one to drift away. Reflect on this Psalm today, and sing a
new song to the Lord. As we worship together, we will be joined
with others from various ethnicities, experiences, and
socioeconomic backgrounds. Despite the differences, Christ
unites us as one body and one Spirit (1 Cor. 12:12-13). We
come together to unite with one voice and celebrate the
goodness and the faithfulness of the Lord. Reflect on the
truthfulness of his word, and refuse to allow anything to deter
you from worshipping him. It will bring peace to your mind and
healing to your soul. Sing praises to Jesus Christ, and let the
beauty of the music be a reminder of the beauty of worshipping
our Lord and Savior.

A Prayer to Start Your Week

*Lord, as I worship you today, I desire to do it all for
your honor and praise. May I never put my trust in
man's word alone, but I desire to trust solely in you. Fill
my heart and soul with the beauty of worshipping you.
Lord, I depend upon you because you alone are faithful
and true, and I rest in your sovereign will. In Jesus'
name, Amen.*

Day 79: Monday's Motivation:

*"I know that you can do all things,
and that no purpose of yours can be thwarted."*—Job 42:2

No Matter What

Everyone wants an explanation for the trials and troubles in this world, whether dealing with a personal struggle or something from a national perspective. We desire that the unexplainable be explained. Our world revolves around understanding, and when faced with the unexpected, we may buckle or become on edge, with no idea why an event happened. We must take our eyes off of the problem and place them on the promise. Job was faced with unexpected calamities in his life. He experienced rejection, pain, tragedy, and had many questions, yet he knew the ONE who is sovereign over all (Job 1:20-23). He understood that God's plan and purpose would be fulfilled in spite of who he was and what he experienced. Know that God's plan will come to pass, no matter what. The severity of the cross of Christ and the beauty of the resurrection is something that continues to keep us in awe and humility. We deserved punishment, but thanks be to God, Christ took our place (Rom. 5:6)! Embrace the truth of the Gospel through faith by surrendering and submitting to the essence and embodiment of truth, Jesus Christ. Despite what comes in life, look to Calvary. Remember, nothing and no one can stop his plan and purpose from coming to fruition. No matter what comes your way, he is the God worth serving.

A Closer Look:

1. Have you ever felt rejected or abandoned? How did you handle those feelings?

2. Consider the character and circumstances surrounding Job. Do you believe you would be able to have the faith he demonstrated?

Day 80: Tuesday's Treasure:

And he said to them, "Follow me,
and I will make you fishers of men."
Immediately they left their nets
and followed him.—Matthew 4:19-20

Purposeful Nets

I believe that within every individual God has given a purpose and a promise. He created us for so much more than mere survival. When making a living is our sole focus, we fail to live the life God sent Jesus to provide for us. Christ came to give all of us lives that would make a difference for eternity. When Jesus called Peter and Andrew, they were making an honest living as fishermen, but Christ saw something greater in them and said, "Follow me." He would teach, train, and disciple them to show people his glory and power, and to develop this life in others. Jesus did not change their profession; he changed their purpose and perspective. They were called to live their lives for an eternal purpose. As Jesus called Peter and Andrew, he is calling you to not live for personal benefit, but to focus on his mission. Christ desires to use you; he wants you to follow him and drop your nets to become fishers of men. When you follow him, it allows you to live a life that is bigger than any reality. Your nets will not be full of useless things and ideas, but they will fulfill the purpose of winning souls for Christ.

A Closer Look:

1. Were you ever asked to do something you felt uncomfortable doing? How did you respond, and how did it make you feel?

2. Do you sense God calling you to a place that seems uncomfortable or challenging? Do you have the faith to step out, or is it still challenging for you?

Day 81: Wednesday's Weapon:

> *And David inquired of the LORD,*
> *"Shall I pursue after this band?*
> *Shall I overtake them?"*
> *He answered him, "Pursue, for you shall surely*
> *overtake and shall surely rescue."*—*1 Samuel 30:8-9*

Questions?

Growing up, I was always encouraged to ask questions. This can be hard when we are unfamiliar with a person or feel uncomfortable asking questions of them. However, desperation for an answer can embolden us to ask anyway. There are other times when decisions are made in haste, simply because an option sounds and feels good. Not so fast, my friend. Be sure that God is at the center (Matt. 6:33). Stand in faith and trust God's voice despite the way the situation appears. Then clear-cut answers will come through God's word for all questions. As David faced the challenge of going against the Amelikites, he asked the right question of the right individual—the Lord—before making a step. Because of this, he was where God desired him to be. He did not walk in fear, but moved in faith as the Lord guided. The unknown is a part of our spiritual journey that requires faith and trusting God's direction (Heb. 11:1). Sometimes God's answers are subtle, so inquire of the Savior and listen closely before making choices. You can't do it alone, so involve him in every detail of life to experience his peace, victory, and joy like never before. Regardless of your questions, he surely has the perfect answer to each one.

A Closer Look:

1. Do you believe it is important to ask questions, or would you rather "figure it out" on your own?

2. Do you find yourself acting based on how you feel, or according to God's word?

Day 82: Thursday's Truth:

But you, O LORD, are a shield about me, my glory,
and the lifter of my head.—Psalm 3:3

Safe and Sound

As a child, I remember going to theme parks and standing in lines to ride what I believed to be some of the most frightening moving attractions in the world. Internally, I didn't want to ride, but I conceded if my grandparents were going. I knew that everything would be fine as long as I stayed close to them. David found himself in a difficult place and began to flee from Absalom, but he knew where to run to find peace (2 Sam. 15). Our modern culture represents some of the most spiritually and morally corrupt times as a nation and world. The threats of persecution and scenes of racial tension and hatred are the headlines on national and local news outlets. During such times, we should run to God rather than running from God or taking matters into our own hands and looking to a person for hope. Although we should stand for justice and truth, ultimately as believers we must run to God for guidance. As David fled, he was reminded of the nature of God. David had to choose between running away in fear, or running to God. You can isolate yourself, become fearful, and blend in with the world, or you can run to God. God will protect you and lift you. Enemies will rise up against you and attack, but God is your shield and sustainer. Jesus is the personification of peace and protection. Rest in who he is and what he is able to do, and experience him in powerful ways. He is for you and will fight for you. Life is a journey, and sometimes the ride is bumpy, but with Christ, it's worth the ride. Reaching our destination, safe and sound, is possible because of victory through Christ.

A Closer Look:

1. When have you felt the most protected? Afraid?

2. How can you depend upon God's word to replace pain and sorrow with comfort and joy?

Day 83: Friday's Freedom:

For I am sure that neither death nor life, nor angels nor rulers,
nor things present nor things to come, nor powers,
nor height nor depth, nor anything in all creation,
will be able to separate us from the love of God
in Christ Jesus our Lord.—Romans 8:38-39

Fully Persuaded

We are confident and sure about a lot of things—the future, our bank accounts, or perhaps the perfect time to get married and have children. As followers of Christ, we sometimes question our relationship with the Lord, leading to uncertainty. Power, prestige, and people cannot validate us, but it's all too easy to create a golden image and begin to worship these "gods." Consider Paul's circumstances. He encountered and endured severe hardships and difficulties, but he made the decision not to fall captive to what might come against him (2 Cor. 11:24-31). Paul could have given up, but he chose not to allow anything to separate him from the love of the Father. Embrace the truth of God's love and experience it; by doing so, nothing can stop you from growing deeper in your relationship with the Lord. Fall so deeply in love with the Father that it leads to submission and obedience in following him. Make the decision today to be fully persuaded so that nothing is a hindrance to drawing closer to the Savior.

A Closer Look:

1. What do you tend to put your trust in? Have these things brought peace to your life?

2. What are some ways you can refuse to allow things to prevent you from experiencing the presence and power of Christ?

Day 84: Saturday's Strength:

Jesus said to him, "I am the way, and the truth, and the life, No one comes to the Father except through me."—John 14:6

The Way

Every four years political campaigns inundate the daily news as politicians cash their ticket to run as the next commander-in-chief of the United States of America. Everyone who seeks to enter the race must meet certain requirements and have a political agenda that serves as the platform for the race they're running. No matter what political party one represents, each individual believes that he or she is the person for the job. Many are criticized or supported because of their standard or lack thereof; we put our trust in them, only to be let down once they are in office. Trust and hope can be placed in the wrong source due to a failure to seek the Lord's guidance (1 Sam. 8:5-10). When choosing a person for President, a business partner, or even a friend, prayerfully consider the person of God's choice. Jesus reminds us that he is THE way, truth, and life. True freedom, peace, and access to the Father are available only through Christ. He came to seek and save the lost, and to pour out his Spirit upon others for God's glory. As followers of Christ, our citizenship is not in this country and world; it is in heaven (Phil. 3:20). The world will let you down, but Jesus, your Lord and Savior, will always hold you up. It is in him that you find the way, the truth, and life in its fullness.

A Closer Look:

1. Do you find yourself trusting in politicians and people more than in God? If so, what can you do to develop total trust in God alone?

2. How can you be more intentional about resting and abiding in the truths of Jesus Christ?

Week 13: Days 85~92

Day 85: Sunday's Celebration:

O LORD, our Lord, how majestic is your name in all the earth! You have set your glory above the heavens.—Psalm 8:1

Badge of Honor

Everyone wants to be known, seen, and heard. In some form or fashion, we like popularity. Society teaches us to seek and give recognition, and this is demonstrated when honoring leaders of all sorts. When the President enters the building, standing applause reflect honor and respect of who he is. We tend to give honor to those deemed worthy because of their accomplishments and status. There is one who outlasts them all; his status is supreme and cannot be matched (Col. 1:15-16). He is the one David speaks of in this Psalm: Our Lord. He is the one who is to be esteemed and exalted. His inexpressible name holds weight and power. Today, celebrate the Savior. Instead of asking God to fill your hands, make the decision today to lift him up above any problems and present realities. Honor the King of kings; he is the center of true joy and the embodiment of all wisdom, glory, and goodness. You can honor those who deserve it, but Jesus Christ is the only one who is truly worthy of a badge of honor.

A Prayer to Start Your Week

Lord, I praise you! Give me more of you today, Lord. I want to experience you in a greater way so that my life will be impacted, allowing me to be of greater influence for your kingdom. Help me to filter all I do through my relationship with you so that my decisions and actions honor you. I want you to be the center of my life, joy, and heart. As I enter worship today, I want to see you. In Jesus' name, Amen.

Day 86: Monday's Motivation:

But they who wait for the LORD shall renew their strength;
they shall mount up with wings like eagles;
they shall run and not be weary;
they shall walk and not faint.—Isaiah 40:31

Just Wait

The word "wait" is foreign in this day and age. It is nearly a curse word. We live in a microwave generation that expects everything immediately, and when that doesn't happen, hope and faith wane. Complaints surface, and some seek illegitimate ways to satisfy desires. Waiting on the sidelines while it seems that everyone else is getting in the game creates discouragement. But don't give up. Stay faithful and keep a sharp focus; your number will be called in due time. The enemy wants you to throw a pity party and ask, "Why me?" God is shaping and molding you so that his will may be complete in you (Phil. 1:6). The prophet Isaiah tells us that there's a blessing and a comfort in faithfully waiting. Waiting doesn't call for you to remain idle but to tread through the treacherous waters while trusting the Lord. This pursuit strengthens and sharpens you during the waiting period as you depend upon the Lord to guide you. Life may not be going the way you envisioned, but don't get lost in the crowd. God's blessings supersede the temporal; they provide strength, endurance, peace, and joy, which are found only in his presence. Sometimes the best action we can take is to just wait.

A Closer Look:

1. We live in a world of instant gratification. Do you think this could be a hindrance to spiritual growth?

2. Why do people in the current culture find it so hard to wait?

3. What do you believe is the blessing in waiting on the Lord?

Day 87: Tuesday's Treasure:

> *But when he came to himself, he said, "How many of my*
> *father's hired servants have more than enough bread,*
> *but I perish here with hunger! I will arise and*
> *go to my father, and I will say to him,*
> *'Father, I have sinned against heaven and before you.*
> *I am no longer worthy to be called your son'...*
> *And he arose and came to the father. But while he was*
> *still a long way off, his father saw him and felt compassion,*
> *and ran and embraced him and kissed him.—Luke 15:17-20*

I'm Better Than This

The freedom and the "right" to make decisions for ourselves are precious rights enjoyed by all Americans. However, the narcissistic society in which we live yields a people who are high on tolerance in an effort not to offend anyone. We've all done things that have gotten us in trouble, whether being disobedient or dishonest, and have found ourselves between a rock and a hard place, needing to be rescued (Isa. 53:6). Your present reality may be as such, but it's important to realize that this doesn't have to be your end. Your heavenly Father has never left you; he's standing with arms wide open. All you have to do is repent and make the decision to intentionally live for Jesus. He loves you too much for you to remain chained in bondage. Make the decision today to turn from the world and run to the Father. True freedom is not the absence of responsibility; it's the love and joy of upholding the standard of Christ. It is never too late! As human beings, it can become easy to believe that life is better outside of the Father's presence. But remember that God created you for a far better purpose than anything you can comprehend.

A Closer Look:

1. Do you believe you are too sinful to come to Christ? Do you believe you can be forgiven?

2. Are there barriers in your life that prevent you from coming back into fellowship with Christ?

Day 88: Wednesday's Weapon:

> *For by wise guidance you can wage your war,*
> *and in abundance of counselors*
> *there is victory.—Proverbs 24:6*

Can I Talk to You?

"Two are better than one." This common phrase holds weight as wars, protests, and organizations have been born and bred through unity, with one mission and purpose: success. In order for these feats to be successful, it takes men and women who have experience and knowledge concerning a particular task or exploit. Solomon pens some encouraging words that I believe are essential for the believer. One in particular is wise guidance. As believers, making decisions apart from the counsel of Godly women and men can create troublesome circumstances. Let us sit at the feet of those who exemplify faith, maturity, and character. God wants us to seek understanding and wisdom, and to run from the idea that we know it all (Prov. 4:7). So, before making the next move in life, first seek the heavenly Father and ask for counsel from those who will empower, edify, and encourage us with truth. Life is better in the context of Godly relationships. This idea of wise counsel has nothing to do with quantity, but speaks solely to quality. Jesus came to earth to model the perfect relationship, not only with our fellow man, but with God the Father as well. Christ submitted to the will of his Father to the point of death on the cross to provide freedom and to model bringing glory to God (Phil. 2:6-8). Our strength lies in unity (Eccl. 4:9). Embrace Godly community and wisdom; without it, there's no victory.

A Closer Look:

1. Identify individuals in your life that you can confide in. Do they hold you accountable for your decisions or celebrate your weaknesses?

2. What are some ways you can be intentional in finding Godly people to hold you accountable?

Day 89: Thursday's Truth:

> *"You shall love the LORD your God with*
> *all your heart and with all your soul and*
> *with all your might."—Deuteronomy 6:5*

Life Worth Living

From time to time, determining our priorities requires brutal honesty while examining our focus. The people and things we love most are what we will make time for, what we will spend our money on, and what we will have a laser focus on (Luke 12:34). Standing at the intersection of right and wrong gives us the choice to satisfy ourselves or to follow God's will. This is no easy task when constantly bombarded with life's issues. Remember that pleasing God becomes a part of your life when filtered through your love for him. You must make sure that you have clear priorities that honor the Lord and that the fire of your passions is kindled by the Holy Spirit. God clears the blurriness that exists and gives you a panoramic perspective of what a life totally submitted to him resembles. Serving and obeying God should be driven by your devotion, not out of a sense of duty. All of your decisions, motives, passions, and thoughts should reflect God's word and character. Love will cost something, but its interest is worth the investment because it is what makes life worth living.

A Closer Look:

1. Is there anything you are tempted to idolize in place of God?

2. Where do you spend most of your time and money?

3. How can you place God at the forefront of all decisions?

Day 90: Friday's Freedom:

> *"Behold, I stand at the door and knock.*
> *If anyone hears my voice and opens the door,*
> *I will come in to him and eat with him*
> *and he with me."*—Revelation 3:20

Promised Truth

These words by Karl Vaters ring with truth: "Jesus never bored people with the Gospel. But entertainment was never the point. Truth was the point. And truth is never boring."[13] In the church at Laodicea, we see a people who were wealthy, yet spiritually bankrupt. Like present-day America, they were the epicenter of comfort and resources. They were a people who "confessed" Christ, but refused to submit to him. What a tragedy! Jesus declared that he was standing at the door, knocking; he desired to dine with them, but it required their humility and total submission. The truth—God's word—is not easily embraced and accepted in today's culture, as well as in many churches across the globe, but it is the key to freedom (John 8:31-32). Embedded within this passage is the truth wedded with grace. Although grace is a free gift, it calls for responsibility on the part of believers (Rom. 6:1-4). Reflecting upon this heart-wrenching passage reveals good news! Although we have all found ourselves straddling the fence, this does not have to be our destination. The doors of the kingdom are open, and seats at the heavenly banquet are available! Through Jesus Christ, truth, authentic love, and freedom flow from him! Be a part of the healthy, vibrant, and Spirit-empowered Church he desires for his children. Submit to and serve the Lord, and proclaim his truth to all the world.

A Closer Look:

1. Why has it become easy in modern culture to find your identity and comfort in material possessions?

2. How can you show others the wonderful truth that true riches are spiritual and come only from the Lord?

Day 91: Saturday's Strength

Now to him who is able to keep you from stumbling
and to present you blameless before the
presence of his glory with great joy, to the only God,
our Savior, through Jesus Christ our Lord,
be glory, majesty, dominion, and authority, before all time
and now and forever. Amen.—Jude 24-25

The Promise

There's assurance in a promise. Deception and being let down are never our heart's desire. Fulfilled promises give us hope, joy, and a sense of peace. Unfortunately, we live in a world where it has become difficult to trust the ones we love. Betrothed couples sign prenuptial agreements; contracts contain ironclad legal wording or opt-out clauses. Because trust can be difficult, it's sometimes easier to put our hope and trust in unhealthy relationships and lifestyles that are contrary to God's will. These choices ultimately place us in bondage and fear. Sadly, this lifestyle becomes the song and rhythm of many lives. The media relies on bad news and "hot topics" to sell papers or to get high viewer ratings, so society has become desensitized to broken promises and false images. But in spite of the present reality, Christ is the one who will ultimately bring joy, peace, and protection (John 14:27). This ultimate joy will not come on the earth, but will come in eternity by our Lord and Savior, Jesus Christ. When this perspective governs your life, it allows you to rest in the power, glory, and authority of God while expectantly waiting for his appearance. He is the one who will be sure to keep you secure and give you endurance for a strong finish. That's a promise.

A Closer Look:

1. Have there been defining moments in your walk with the Lord when he has rescued you?

2. Where have you felt God's protection in those defining moments?

Day 92: Sunday's Celebration:

"Go therefore and make disciples of all nations, baptizing them in the name of the Father and of the Son and of the Holy Spirit, teaching them to observe all that I have commanded you. And behold, I am with you always, to the end of the age."—Matthew 28:19-20

Go Forth

It is a blessing to be in the company of someone whose presence changes the atmosphere by challenging one to live a life that is beyond them, shaped by the Gospel. This is what Jesus' ministry demonstrated. At the end of his ministry on earth, he left life-changing words with his disciples and challenged them to go outside their comfort zone and expose all people to the Gospel. Even today, this commission continues to be a clarion call. But if our churches are merely weekly gatherings without evangelism and intentional discipleship, they simply become entertainment venues. Through the work of the Holy Spirit, we have the awesome privilege and responsibility to expand the Gospel of Jesus Christ to all people (Acts 1:8). So eagerly accept Christ's calling while waiting in joyful anticipation of that day of celebration when we will all be gathered around the throne (Rev. 7:9). Stay rooted in Christ and go forth to fulfill this glorious calling as his Bride.

A Prayer to Start Your Week

Lord, make me an instrument of your peace. Where there is hatred, let me sow love; where there is injury, pardon; where there is doubt, faith; where there is despair, hope; where there is darkness, light; where there is sadness, joy. O, Divine Master, grant that I may not so much seek to be consoled as to console; to be understood as to understand; to be loved as to love; For it is in giving that we receive; it is in pardoning that we are pardoned; it is in dying that we are born again to eternal life. In Jesus' name, Amen.[14]—St. Francis of Assisi Prayer

A Challenge and a Call to Action

Living a Christian life and being the light that Christ desires each of his followers to be starts with faith, but our faith needs to be lived out and strengthened (James 2:17). Make a daily commitment to pray, read God's Holy word, and meditate upon his precepts. As we grow spiritually and faithfully serve as ambassadors and servants in the earth, we are pointing people to the one who made salvation possible, our Lord and Savior, Jesus Christ.

The simple yet heartfelt words in the precious old hymn, *Day by Day, Dear Lord, of Thee Three Things I Pray*, were written centuries ago. Yet just as Jesus Christ is the same yesterday, today, and forever, these profound lyrics will be true forevermore (Heb. 13:8). The lyrics beautifully state the concepts of faithfulness and daily hungering for a closer walk with Jesus Christ.

Day by day, day by day,
O, dear Lord, three things I pray:
to see thee more clearly, love thee more dearly,
follow thee more nearly, day by day.[15]

So here is my challenge, and a call to action for all believers. Allow these sacred words to seep into your hearts, illuminate your minds, and renew your souls. Be inspired to see the Lord more clearly, love him more dearly, and follow him more nearly, day by day.

Acknowledgements

This book would not be possible without the permission and promise of my Lord and Savior, Jesus Christ, to whom all glory and honor belong.

To my wife, Shantel, thank you for your loving support and encouragement. You are truly a blessing in my life, and the perfect helpmate, a true gift from the Lord.

To my parents and grandparents, thanks for your support, encouragement, Godly wisdom, and prayers. For your wonderful Christian example of living a life that is faithful and steadfastly centered on Jesus Christ, I am forever grateful to you.

To my brother, Tarick, you are an all-star. You will change the world for God's glory!

I want to thank the administration, my professors, and the staff of Beeson Divinity School for their superb, exceptional, and anointed leadership and theological training. Thank you for being an institution that submits to the authority of Scripture and for your heart for the Church of Jesus Christ I am forever indebted to you. Beeson exemplifies the heart of the Gospel, without compromise.

There are several special people I would like to thank for their leadership, heart for the Gospel, character, and integrity. Because of the time they have invested, they have had a tremendous influence and an eternal spiritual impact upon my life.

To Dr. Lyle W. Dorsett, through your leadership, example and wisdom, I was encouraged to write this devotional. I will always remember and hold dear the principles you taught me. To Mr. Armstead Herndon, your wisdom, example, and dedication to the cause of Christ are extraordinary. Both of you were an inspiration to me in writing this book, and I will always treasure our many conversations.

To Bishop Raymond W. Johnson, thank you for recognizing and affirming God's hand upon my life years ago. Your leadership and impact have blessed my life and ministry.

To Pastor and Mrs. Wuan D. Miller, thank you for your Godly example, wisdom and encouragement. You both are truly a blessing in my life.

To Bishop Gregory Cooper, Sr., thank you for your guidance and example to the body of Christ.

I am eternally grateful for each of you, and I count you as dear friends and fellow soldiers for the cause of Christ. My sincere prayer is that I will rise to the level of outstanding mentorship and Godly examples all of you have been.

To my students, God has chosen and called you to live a life for his glory alone. Continue living for him and serving him wholeheartedly. You are the NOW generation.

To all my other spiritual mentors, too numerous to name, who have embodied the true essence of character and integrity before me and deposited spiritual truth and Godly wisdom even to this day, I am forever indebted to you. In the words of the Apostle Paul, "I thank my God in all my remembrance of you, always in every prayer of mine for you all making my prayer with joy, because of your partnership in the gospel from the first day until now."—Philippians 1:3-5

A Message From the Author

Thank you for reading my book! It is my sincere prayer that the words here have inspired you to seek a closer relationship with Jesus Christ. I also pray that the book allowed you to really think about your Christian walk and provided many ideas for ways in which you can live the Godly life that the Lord would have you to live while being of service to your fellow Christians, family, friends, neighbors, and to the world.

If you enjoyed the book, please take just a moment to go to Amazon.com and leave a review. I would be so grateful. Thank you very much.

Pastor Trey

About the Author

 Trailon D. Johnson, known as Trey, is a pastor, teacher, mentor, and 21st century leader with a passion for sharing the Gospel of Jesus Christ and serving as a shepherd to disciple fellow believers. A native of Baton Rouge, Louisiana, Trey attended Birmingham-Southern College in Birmingham, Alabama, where he received a Bachelor of Arts degree in Religion. He furthered his theological studies to earn a Master of Divinity degree from Beeson Divinity School at Samford University, also in Birmingham. He plans to pursue doctoral work in the future.

Recently married, Trey and his beautiful, loving wife Shantel enjoy traveling, spending time with family, and sharing the gospel of Christ. Trey and Shantel share a deep commitment to promoting faith in Jesus Christ, and their greatest desire as a ministry team is to impact the local church, community, and world with the gospel of Christ, and to disciple men and women to live fruitful and God-honoring lives for the cause of Christ. *Soli Deo Gloria!*

Trey's current literary plans include writing several additional devotional books in the *Day by Day* series, which he believes will offer something for everyone. Future plans for other books on a variety of spiritual topics are in the works as well, so stay tuned!

For more information or to book Pastor Trey for speaking and ministry engagements, please contact him via email at info@tdjohnsonministries.org.

And this is eternal life, that they know you the only true God, and Jesus Christ whom you have sent.—John 17:3

End Notes

Introduction:

[1] Gene Fant, "Our Hearts Are Restless," December 3, 2009, *First Things*, *http://www.firstthings.com/blogs/firstthoughts/2009/12/our-hearts-are-restless.*

[2] "Heart Disease Facts," Heart Disease, Last updated August 10, 2015, *Centers for Disease Control and Prevention*, *http://www.cdc.gov/heartdisease/facts.htm.*

Day 2:

[3] Lyle W. Dorsett, *Serving God and Country: U.S. Military Chaplains in World War II*, (New York: Penguin Group, 2012), 3.

Day 5:

[4] "My Hope Is Built," Lyrics by Edward Mote, circa 1834, Public domain, *http://www.hymntime.com/tch/htm/m/y/h/myhopeis.htm.*

Day 9:

[5] Joseph Luciani, "Why 80 Percent of New Year's Resolutions Fail," *U.S. News & World Report: Health*, December 29, 2015, *U.S. News & World Report*, http://health.usnews.com/health-news/blogs/eat-run/articles/2015-12-29/why-80-percent-of-new-years-resolutions-fail, (Accessed March 15, 2016).

Day 19:

[6] C.S. Lewis, *Mere Christianity*, (New York: Harper One, 1952), 136-7.

Day 20:

[7] Charles Wesley, "O, for a Thousand Tongues to Sing," 1739, Public Domain. *Hymnary*, *http://www.hymnary.org/text/o_for_a_thousand_tongues_to_sing_my.*

Day 26:

[8] Katherine Muniz, "20 ways Americans are blowing their money," March 24, 2014, *USA Today*, *http://www.usatoday.com/story/money/personalfinance/2014/03/24/20-ways-we-blow-our-money/6826633.*

Day 31:

[9] "Hunger Facts," *Stop Hunger Now*, tp://www.stophungernow.org/learn/hunger-facts.

Day 49:

[10] Horatio G. Spafford, "It Is Well with My Soul," 1873, Public Domain, *Timeless Truths*, http://library.timelesstruths.org/music/It_Is_Well_with_My_Soul.

Day 50:

[11] Edward Perronet, "All Hail the Power of Jesus' Name," 1780, Public Domain, *Hymnary*, *http://www.hymnary.org/text/all_hail_the_power_of_jesus_name_let*.

Day 60:

[12] War Room, dir. Alex Kendrick, perf. Priscilla C. Shirer, T.C. Stallings, and Karen Abercrombie, FaithStep Films, Affirm Films, Red Sky Studios, 2015.

Day 90:

[13] Karl Vaters, "The Church Does Not Exist To Entertain Us—Or Bore Us," *Pivot: A Blog by Karl Vaters, Christianity Today Leadership Journal*, *http://www.christianitytoday.com/karl-vaters/2016/april/church-does-not-exist-to-entertain-us-or-bore-us.html* (April 1, 2016).

Day 92

[14] "Peace Prayer of St. Francis of Assisi," *Saints, Catholic News Agency*, *http://www.catholicnewsagency.com/resources/saints/saints/peace-prayer-of-st-francis-of-assisi/*.

A Challenge and a Call to Action:

[15] *Day by Day, Dear Lord, of Thee Three Things I Pray*, attributed to Richard of Chichester, (b. 1197, d. 1253), Public Domain. *http://www.hymnary.org/text/day_by_day_dear_lord*.

Made in the USA
San Bernardino, CA
19 December 2016